IDENTIFYING HEART TRANSFORMATION

IDENTIFYING HEART TRANSFORMATION

Exploring Different Kinds of Human Change

Nate Brooks

ISBN
Paper: 978-1-63342-291-9
epub: 978-1-63342-292-6
Kindle: 978-1-63342-293-3

Shepherd Press
P.O. Box 24
Wapwallopen, PA 18660

www.shepherdpress.com

COUNSEL FOR THE HEART
A RESOURCE for WORD-BASED TRANSFORMATION and PRACTICAL DISCIPLESHIP

Cover design by www.greatwriting.org
Typography by **documen**. www.documen.co.uk
Printed in USA

Endorsements

Can you be good but not connected to Jesus? Absolutely. That is fine news for people who avoid Jesus, but, if we assume that we follow him, this is reason to look carefully at our hearts. Nate takes us through some necessary theology, then helps us discern what it looks like for us to be *in Christ*.

Ed Welch
Faculty Member, Christian Counseling & Educational Foundation

Nate Brooks brings the big concepts of theology to the hard question, "How exactly do people change?" I particularly appreciate how he avoids simple platitudes that make Christian change seem easy or non-Christian change seem impossible. *Identifying Heart Transformation* is like an accessible conversation with Jonathan Edwards' *Religious Affections* in everyday language with relatable examples. We need more reflections on important questions like this one.

Brad Hambrick
Pastor of Counseling, The Summit Church
Assistant Professor of Biblical Counseling, Southeastern Baptist Theological Seminary

Identifying Heart Transformation offers invaluable clarity on how and why people change, vital concepts for Christian ministry. Nate Brooks uses concrete illustrations and biblical examples that help unpack and make operational complex theological truths about our hearts and what motivates them. It is critical to distinguish between changes born from self-effort and transformation brought about by God's work in a human heart if we want to recognize and appeal to God's gracious work in ourselves and others. Your own heart and ministry will benefit greatly from this work.

Darby Strickland
Faculty Member, Christian Counseling & Educational Foundation

A talented author can take something complex and make it simple; a gifted author can take something that looks simple and show the complexity of it without overwhelming the reader. That is what I appreciate about Nate's latest book which takes a topic like change and unpacks it from a variety of angles. In doing so, he expands our understanding of change and how it is accomplished. I'm certain this readable and accessible work will increase our clarity and wisdom in helping every believer become mature in Christ.

Jonathan Holmes
Executive Director, Fieldstone Counseling

Every Christian wants to see godly change in their life, but we often struggle with how that actually happens. In this wise and insightful book, Nate Brooks takes the reader on a deep journey into the one place where the deepest kind of change begins: the human heart. By peeling away misconceptions and misunderstandings of the way the heart works, this book leaves the reader with renewed hope that God-honoring change is possible through the power of God's grace. It will be a great blessing to the church.

Mike Kruger
President and Samuel C. Patterson Professor of New Testament and Early Christianity, Reformed Theological Seminary, Charlotte

Change is an essential aspect of the counseling process and the Christian life. But what kind of change are we looking for? How do we monitor and measure that change? Is change possible only for Christians or do unbelievers change too? If both change, how do we know that the change we see is rooted in the gospel and empowered by the Spirit? These are the deep and nuanced questions Brooks addresses in *Identifying Heart Transformation*. He brings years of counseling and deep theological wisdom together in this excellent and accessible resource.

Curtis Solomon
Executive Director, Biblical Counseling Coalition

As a seminary professor and counselor, I know how this book by Nate Brooks is so needed. He carefully articulates not only important nuances in our personhood but also different types of change between believers and unbelievers, as well as how we might determine when real change has taken root. And yet, this book is easy to understand, bolstered by personal stories that connect the reader both to Nate and to the concepts he's explaining. This is an excellent text—it will be required reading in my counseling class from here on out.

Kristin Kellen
Assistant Professor of Biblical Counseling, Southeastern Baptist Theological Seminary

In *Identifying Heart Transformation*, Nate Brooks offers a biblically rich and practical approach to heart transformation. He has helpfully explained categories for change that endures while also acknowledging the challenges we all face in our sanctification. I am eager to read this book with counselees and members of our church, because it provides a template for discussing our need for softness of heart and perseverance in our journey of faith. We should all add this book to our list of essential discipleship resources.

Beth Broom
LPC Supervisor, CCTS-I, and Director, Christian Trauma Healing Network

Identifying Heart Transformation answers difficult questions about how people change in concise and easy-to-understand language. This book challenged me to consider the true depth of my own heart change and offered me tools for assessing change in the people I counsel. Truly a helpful resource!

Esther Smith
LCPC, and author, *The Whole Life*

Dr. Nate Brooks has provided the reader with thoroughly biblical and helpful categories. At times, we can talk past one another regarding change, the nature of people, and discerning true change, and we need clear, biblical definitions and categories. Dr. Brooks provides clarifying categories of anthropology and sanctification in a way that sets the stage to better understand

and help people. This important work provides clarity on the human heart and change in a way you, perhaps, have not seen until now.

Greg Gifford
Associate Professor of Biblical Counseling, The Master's University

A growing understanding of the human experience is essential to providing wise counsel and care. In *Identifying Heart Transformation*, Nate Brooks offers a robust understanding of the inner person and of the different ways that people change. He differentiates between change that is wrought by grace and change that is fashioned through self-effort alone. And he gives hope for true and lasting change. Those who offer care and counsel to God's people will benefit from these insights.

Greg Wilson, LCP Supervisor, and author, *When Home Hurts*

Through sound doctrine and powerful illustration, Nate Brooks gives needed clarity to one of the most important concepts in all of biblical counseling. Here is a book that has the potential to strengthen anyone's counseling.

Dave and Krista Dunham
Authors, *Table for Two: Biblical Counsel for Eating Disorders*

Identifying Heart Transformation analyzes the phenomenon of real change that is common across the human experience. Brooks draws from common-sense reality and inerrant Scripture in order to provide readers a well-reasoned explanation of the types of change that occur within both Christians and their unbelieving neighbors. His delineation is convincing. His exegesis is compelling.

Jenny Solomon
Author, *Restore Your Marriage*

To Alethea,

Who didn't exist and thus missed the cutoff for the last dedication,
But now has captured my heart in ways I didn't know possible.

Contents

Acknowledgments

"No man is an island entire of itself; every man is a piece of the continent, a part of the main," wrote the English poet John Donne. Books follow humanity in this form, and this book would not exist without the aid of many of God's people.

The draft version of this manuscript was far inferior to the finished product, and I have Jenny Solomon, Jonathan Homesley, Clair Northcutt, and Dave and Krista Dunham to thank for their careful reading and helpful critiques. My "Methods of Biblical Change" students at Reformed Theological Seminary, Charlotte have likewise served as a collective guinea pig for this project, and I'm indebted to their lively minds, kind affirmations, and patient longsuffering.

Listing everyone who contributed to this project by personal influence would be a book in and of itself, but I'd be remiss not to mention how grateful I am for my faithful pastor/mentor John Marc Wiemann, my mentor/friend Jeremy Pierre, and my parents, who introduced me to Jesus Christ, the one who changed my heart. Thank you to Bon Iver, Taylor Swift, The Wailin' Jennys, and Hans Zimmer for providing the epic and angsty soundtrack this geriatric millennial needed to write something compelling.

Saving the best for last, I'm grateful for my treasures—Kate, Blaise, Gresham, and Alethea—whose love is far sweeter than the joy of having a book published. And, as always, no amount of faithful conversation, friendship, and editing would be sufficient to hold me back from all error, and whatever errors or untruths have seeped into this work are mine alone. I pray you are as blessed by this book as I have been in writing it.

Nate Brooks
Charlotte, NC

Foreword

No one is master of his own heart. And most of the time, no one cares to be.

All of us tend to move through life responding in whatever way comes naturally, then figuring *that's just the way I am*. We go along like this for quite some time, acting and reacting moment by moment without much reflection as to why.

But then occasionally we get a glimpse of where this way of responding takes us. Every now and then, we realize our behaviors have fallen into patterns we don't like. We know we ought to clean up our language or use our time better or treat our families with more kindness, but we don't. Not just our behaviors, but our thoughts and emotions can fall into patterns we don't like. Depression can cloud our entire mental horizon, anxiety can strain our tired minds, rage can rise up without any discernible reason. It's just true. One of the plainest but most perplexing things about each of us is that we can be dissatisfied with *our own* responses.

So we decide to change.

But it takes only a few hours of trying for us to realize we can't. Who am I kidding? It takes only a few *moments* to realize we can't simply decide in a moment to change such deeply established patterns of response. We know our words come from our own mouths, our thoughts occur in our own heads, and our tears flow from our own eyes. We know all these responses to be *ours* and not *someone else's*. Yet we realize we have little control over what's deep down inside us, let alone how it comes brimming to the surface. No one is master of his own heart.

That's because someone else is. Someone else is responsible for both its design and its redemption. He alone knows its original blueprint. He alone knows the cost of its renovation. Jesus Christ is Master of the human heart, twice over. As Creator, he made it. He structured this godlike design into every human to ever live. As Savior, he redeems it. He fulfilled God's righteous design for human life for anyone who trusts in him.

In this book, Nate Brooks helps you sort out this double mastery of Jesus over the human heart.

Jesus is Master of the human heart by right of being its Creator. Nate describes how all people everywhere are designed to reflect the personhood of God. They were made to respond to life with thoughts, desires, and choices that no other creature is capable of. This is the privilege of being human. Even with all the disruption brought about by humankind's fall into sin, this core design still holds true. Nate describes how change can occur in anyone because of this gracious, ongoing reality: all people are designed to be like God, and Jesus is the Master of them all. He shows his mastery in his common grace works for their *common* good in this life, including real change that may occur through a number of different means.

Jesus is Master of the human heart by right of being its Redeemer. Nate also describes how Jesus shows his fullest mastery only over those who recognize him as Master, who belong to him by faith. This mastery is even more gracious—not just common grace for their common good, but special grace for their *ultimate* good, in this life and the one to come. This is the highest form of heart change, the kind of new life that changes a person's fundamental identity and determines his or her eternal destiny. This highest form of mastery brings about the highest form of life: being like Jesus Christ.

Nate will describe both kinds of change as an expression of God's multi-varied grace to humanity in general and to his redeemed people in particular. God shows both common and special grace through different *means*. Nate will explain that common grace and special grace are *complementary* and not *competitive*, allowing us to explore the question of *how* they complement each other in the change process.

But like any adventure, this exploration has its dangers and its gains. Nate is an excellent guide because he hunts for the gains while being aware of the dangers. You will find that he demonstrates a calm confidence in the Word of God as he engages with sources of knowledge outside of Scripture. This will help you grow in your own ability to practice the best kind of discernment. Not a defensive, furrow-browed discernment that sees only danger and not gain. Not a naive, wide-eyed discernment that sees only the gain and not the danger. Rather, he will build the kind of discernment that humbly, even joyfully, recognizes the mystery of God's common grace scattered throughout a world that nevertheless needs the special grace of God for its complete redemption.

It is this kind of discernment that best leads Christians forward, confident that the eternal truths of Scripture sufficiently and effectively frame our understanding of the changing experiences of people. Ultimately, it is this kind of discernment that honors the twice-lordship of Jesus Christ.

I trust you will find your own heart warmed as Nate points you to Jesus, the Master of the human heart. And the Master of yours.

Jeremy Pierre

Part I

Mapping a Human Being

1 Four Windows

If a stranger were to step into my church, and probably yours as well, they would quickly realize that Christians care a great deal about something called the "soul." They would hear us find our identity in Jesus' relationship with us as we sing, "Jesus, lover of my soul." Griefs and sorrows are met with a chorus of "It is well with my soul," and we remind our anxious selves, "Be still, my soul, the Lord is on your side."

The pastor's sermon may very well touch on a passage urging Christians to fear not those who can kill the body, but the one who can destroy both body and soul. Or perhaps the message might center around the psalmist's cry, "Why are you downcast, O my soul?" Should our visitor be an unbeliever, before long they would encounter the Christian practice of evangelism, which not too long ago was commonly referred to as "soulwinning." Any Christian funeral displays that ever-so-hard-to-describe mingling of grief and joy over the fact that though our loved one's body is decaying, their "soul is with the Lord."

Mankind as Body and Soul

For most of human history, it was hardly controversial to say that part of being human is to have an unseen, inner person. Many Christian beliefs have stood apart as odd to unbelievers over the ages, but the concept that people have a soul has historically not been one of them. Times change. Singing "Jesus, lover of my soul" asserts something that is now quite controversial: not that

Jesus loves your soul, but that you have one at all. Writing for the American Psychological Association, Bruce Wampold insists that "one of the cornerstones of modern scientific medicine is materialism, a philosophical term that stipulates that matter is the sole basis of reality."[1] This perspective certainly runs counter to Christian teaching on the human person.

Church history is full of helpful documents that lend us a hand by bringing clarity to what the church has taught throughout the ages regarding the human person. The time-honored Second Helvetic Confession describes us this way: "Man consists of two different substances in one person: an immortal soul which, when separate from the body, neither sleeps nor dies, and a mortal body which will nevertheless be raised up from the dead at the last judgment, in order that then the whole man, either in life or in death, abide forever."[2]

The basis of the claim that man "consists of two different substances in one person" can be seen throughout the Bible. It is particularly clear in Jesus' warning, referred to above, not to fear those who kill the *body* but are not able to kill the *soul* (Matt. 10:28). Both the body and the soul are real, both are essential parts of who we are as people, and they are not the same thing.

God created both the body and the soul, but he created them at different times. Genesis 2:7 states, "Then the LORD God formed the man out of the dust from the ground and breathed the breath of life into his nostrils, and the man became a living being [lit. "soul"]." The soul and the body are not both made of earth, but rather are of two different substances. First, man's body is formed out of the dust, and then the soul comes into existence as God's breath of life fills that lifeless body. Together, the body and the soul make up a human person.

The Soul as the Center of the Person

Having two of something requires figuring out the relationship between them. Is the human person a household of equals, or does the body or the soul claim primacy? Far from agreeing with contemporary culture's idea that the body is the most important aspect of who we are, the Bible teaches that our souls are the center of our personhood.

The Bible shows the primacy of the soul in several ways. We have already seen that the body existed without the soul, yet was not considered a human being until the soul was created. Due to Adam and Eve's disobedience, our bodies will one day taste death and lie decomposing in the ground until the Lord's return. Yet even though our bodies will be dead, our souls live and are present with God after our mortal life has drawn to a close (2 Cor. 5:1–8). The body is clearly a part of us, but it is secondary because it can be dead and we still be alive as persons with the Lord.

Two more biblical truths highlight the fact that our souls are the center of who we are. First, we are made alive in Christ as his Spirit regenerates our souls.[3] Although our bodies will be made new, that event is still future and will occur only at the final resurrection. In the meantime, every Christian feels the tension of being half alive and half decaying as our regenerated souls are not matched by regenerated flesh and blood. Second, the Bible consistently draws a distinction between worship conducted by the body and worship conducted by the soul. One need only think of Cain, the faithless Israelites in the Promised Land, or Ananias and Sapphira to see that obedient actions were rejected because something was amiss within the worshipper's soul.

Puritan pastor and theologian Thomas Watson rightly spoke of the soul as "the man of the man … the diamond in the ring."[4] Although our bodies are an important aspect of who we are as people, the centrality of the soul highlights where we should begin in our study of change. The deepest change a person can experience happens in their soul because the soul is the core of who they are.

A Whirlwind of Terms for the Inner Person[5]

Thus far, we have used the term "soul" to refer to our immaterial substance, our inner person. This is rather odd for a book entitled *Identifying Heart Transformation*. How exactly do we get to the heart if the soul of the person is the center of who we are? Are we not already straying from the map by focusing on something other than the soul?

These questions cause us to study hard how the Bible talks about our immaterial substance. Surveying the text of Scripture reveals that the Bible uses a number of different terms in order to describe our inner person, the most common of which are *soul*, *spirit*, *mind*, and *heart*. Each of these simultaneously overlaps with the others and carries a slightly different view of what our inner person is. Each term may be thought of as a window that allows us to see a different snapshot of something that—at its core—is rather a mystery to us.

I grew up attending very minor-league stock car races in rural Washington State with my grandparents. The events were small enough that before the races, we would walk into the pits and talk to the drivers. One driver even had me autograph the hood of her car. Eventually, we would climb into the metal grandstands and watch drivers jockey for position to be the first to take the checkered flag. The next morning, we would walk the track and pick up twisted chunks of fiberglass shed by crashing cars the night before.

Each of these experiences gave me greater understanding of race cars. I began to grasp the importance of aerodynamics by running my hand across smooth sheet metal carefully tailored to slip through the air. I felt in my chest the power of the engines as two dozen drivers mashed their accelerators in unison at the drop of the green flag. I appreciated the strong forces which ripped cars apart by holding in my hands debris from the night before.

Each of these encounters was a true and real observation of a race car. However, the multifaceted way in which I experienced them helped me appreciate and understand far more than one of those experiences alone. Similarly, the Bible's use of many terms for our immaterial inner person gives us a richer portrait of who we are than one solitary term ever could. Understanding the nuances of how each term is used within Scripture will help us make sense of what's going on inside of us, and of how we may change.

Term #1: Soul

The first window that we may peer through to observe our inner person is the term "soul." As we've already seen, this term is the first one used within Scripture to describe humans as living beings.[6] We noted above how, after God formed Adam's body from the dust of the ground, he "breathed the breath of life into his nostrils, and the man became a living being [lit. "a living soul"]" (Gen. 2:7).

"Soul" is often used throughout the Scriptures to specifically refer to man's immaterial substance, the opposite side of the coin from our bodies. The focus of "soul" on a person's aliveness can be seen in Jesus' words in Matthew 6:25: "Therefore I tell you: Don't worry about your life [lit. "soul"], what you will eat or what you will drink; or about your body, what you will wear. Isn't life [lit. "soul"] more than food and the body more than clothing?"

The writers of Scripture often use "soul" to stand for the entirety of their inner person. The psalmist inquires of himself, "Why, my soul, are you so dejected? Why are you in such turmoil? Put your hope in God, for I will still praise him, my Savior and my God" (Ps. 42:5). Job similarly declares, "I will complain in the bitterness of my soul" (Job 7:11). Jesus offers comfort to hurting and fading people by assuring them, "Take up my yoke and learn from me, because I am lowly and humble in heart, and you will find rest for your souls" (Matt. 11:29). This use of "soul" makes a good deal of sense as the term speaks of our aliveness as people. Only living things grow weary, experience sadness, and receive comfort.

Term #2: Spirit

The term "spirit" provides a second view into our inner person. "Soul" and "spirit" sound quite similar to our ears, to the point that we often think of them as being interchangeable. Yet this window is set just off to the side of "soul," giving us a slightly different view into who we are as people. While "soul" speaks to our aliveness, "spirit" highlights how human beings are related to God.[7]

As Jesus stood at the precipice of death on the cruel Roman cross, he cried out, "Father, into your hands I entrust my spirit" (Luke 23:46). Jesus is clearly referring to the immaterial part of himself, in contrast to his battered body which would soon occupy Joseph of Arimathea's tomb. In this highly relational moment, Jesus chooses the term "spirit," highlighting his relationship to the Father.

Elsewhere, Paul urges the Philippian believers to "[stand] firm in one spirit ... contending together for the faith of the gospel" (Phil. 1:27). He charges Timothy to be courageous, as "God has not given us a spirit of fear, but one of power, love, and sound judgment" (2 Tim. 1:7). He likewise closes some of his letters with a benediction asking that "the grace of the Lord Jesus Christ be with your spirit" (Phil. 4:23; cf. 2 Tim. 4:22). Each of these contexts focuses on the special relationship human beings have with God himself. We are not inert rocks or spiritually mute dolphins, but covenantal creatures who live before the face of God.

Term #3: Mind

The third window is provided by the term "mind." While "soul" and "spirit" sound otherworldly and inaccessible, "mind" shifts our focus by sounding far more grounded in our daily life. We *don't* directly experience ourselves as ethereal, immaterial substances. We *do* know what it's like to think, reason, and form ideas within our heads.

The Bible's use of "mind," however, is much broader than simply referring to thought or reason. Like "soul" and "spirit," "mind" refers to the whole of our inner person. Those who have rejected God are described as being given over to a "corrupt mind" (Rom. 1:28). Paul urges the Christians in Rome to be "transformed by the renewing of your mind" (Rom. 12:2). In one of the most hopeful passages in the Bible, he tells the Corinthian believers, "We have the mind of Christ" (1 Cor. 2:16).

"Mind" highlights our ability to reason. We are not irrational creatures. The Lord is able to tell errant Israel, "Come now, let us reason together" (Isa. 1:18 ESV) because he has made people to be able to weigh and consider who he is and what he says. We are not "irrational animals" (Jude 1:10), but those who have the necessary rational capacity to engage in a conscious relationship with God. Not only is our inner person alive (soul) and in relationship with God (spirit), it also vibrantly hums with concrete, propositional interpretations of everything around us. Because we *are* mind, we reason and think.

Term #4: Heart

The fourth major term that Scripture uses to refer to our inner person is "heart." This window provides us a glimpse of how our inner person has a moral orientation. "Heart" is frequently paired with other terms and phrases to indicate its morality. Morally speaking, we are not blank slates, but are inclined toward or away from God and his righteousness.

All but a handful of human beings perished beneath the God-appointed waves of Noah's day because "the wickedness of man was great in the earth, and . . . every intention of the thoughts of his heart was only evil continually" (Gen. 6:5 ESV). This great purging of the wicked did not change human nature, however, and well over a millennium later Jeremiah would again write, "The heart is more deceitful than anything else, and incurable" (Jer. 17:9).

The Bible portrays the great change that takes place within us through salvation in terms of the heart. All who believe have experienced "circumcision . . . of the heart" (Rom. 2:29). The Holy Spirit resides "in our hearts as a down payment" (2 Cor. 1:22), and one day those who are "pure in heart . . . will see God" (Matt. 5:8). More than any other term for our inner person, "heart" is used to refer to the person's *moral* stance before God.

Since it is the term that highlights our morality, "heart" is also often used as the origin point for our thoughts, desires, and choices. We will look more at this later, but for now Mark 7:21–22 makes the point clear: "For from within, out of people's hearts, come evil thoughts, sexual immoralities, thefts, murders, adulteries, greed, evil actions, deceit, self-indulgence, envy, slander, pride, and foolishness." The toxic cocktail of evil thoughts, evil lusts and desires, and evil actions proceeds from the heart. The heart is thus the moral and functional center of the human person.

Four Terms and an Opportunity for Confusion

All four of these terms serve to highlight different aspects of our inner person. Because each of these terms has a different flavor, sometimes the mistake has been made to view them as referring to different parts of the human person. Soul and spirit are sometimes thought of as being different pieces within us, meaning that a human being is made of three substances (along with the body) instead of two. Mind and heart are often set against each other, with "mind" referring to our intellect and "heart" referring to our desires and feelings.

Indeed, there are places in the Scriptures that might seem to suggest that each of these terms refers to a different part of us. The Greatest Commandment serves as an example, where Jesus states that people are to "love the Lord your God with all your heart, with all your soul, and with all your mind" (Matt. 22:36–40). All in all, the Bible pairs heart and mind together twenty-one times, and soul and spirit are paired three times.[8]

To make sense of this, we need to remember that there are different ways to understand terms used side by side. Sometimes we use two terms to refer to two different things or ideas. If we're at the table and I ask you to pass the pepper and the salt, I am asking you to pass two different seasonings my way. Other times we use multiple terms to provide emphasis and drive home our point. When a father looks at the food bill and tells four teenage sons, "You're going to eat me out of house and home!" he is using the terms "house" and "home" as synonyms.

It is the second of these two options that the Bible embraces as it uses these terms together. A. Craig Troxel helpfully writes, "The heart includes and encompasses the mind with all its cognitive abilities, like reasoning, meditating, remembering, and believing. This is why the words 'heart' and 'mind' often appear together in Scripture. In such instances, they are not being contrasted but coordinated."[9]

The Bible uses the terms "heart," "soul," "mind," and "spirit" in coordination with one another and not in contrast. Returning to the Greatest Commandment (Matt. 22:36–40), we can clearly see that Jesus is emphasizing how people must love God with all they are—made even clearer by the fact that "spirit" is left off the list. He is not cataloging different aspects of who we are, but rather saying that the love of God must be woven through all of us.

Coordinating Terms and Change

If we start with a wrong road map of the human person, it will ultimately lead to confusion about how we may be transformed. This becomes evident if we mistakenly see the various terms used within the Bible as chopping our inner man up into different pieces.

Consider, for instance, what happens when you mislabel

the heart as standing for man's desires and feelings rather than his whole inner person. The Bible's insistence that the heart is deceitful above all things (Jer. 17:9) suddenly means that our emotions are far more disordered than our reason. Our lives would then be troubled mainly because we have let our reason fall under the sway of our feelings. Personal and spiritual growth would primarily consist of growing in knowledge and rationality, something clearly not taught by Scripture (James 4:17).

Other troubles arise when we mislabel the heart as standing for a person's desires and feelings rather than for the whole inner man. What should we make of the fact that "[God] has also put his seal on us and given us the Spirit in our hearts as a down payment" (2 Cor. 1:22)? If "heart" means our emotions, then this passage would be teaching that the Spirit's guidance is primarily experienced through our desires and emotions. How is this to be if godliness is connected with reason? Wrongly labeling the heart thus leads to chaos.

Rightly understanding change is dependent upon rightly understanding what is being changed. Restoring heart, soul, mind, and spirit to their proper places as equivalent terms will bring clarity to understanding how change occurs. Each term has its own unique texture, giving us insight into who we are. However, at their core, each synonymously refers to our immaterial, inner person.

Why "Identifying Heart Transformation"?

A quite natural question arises at this point. If "heart," "soul," "mind," and "spirit" are synonyms, why isn't this book titled *Identifying Soul Transformation* or *Identifying Mind Transformation*? This good question gets at why we use certain terms in certain situations. Although "soul," "spirit," "mind," and "heart" all refer to the inner person, they are all most properly used in slightly different ways.

Think for a moment about how we introduce people to one another. There are many terms that I can and do use to refer to my spouse. "Kate" is her name and refers to her as an individual person. "Wife" highlights her connectivity to me. "Mommy" highlights her relationship with our children.

If I'm introducing my wife to you, I can refer to her in ways that are entirely true but yet are discordant in that particular situation. You would find it odd if I gestured toward her and said, “This is Lisa’s daughter.” While my wife is Lisa’s daughter, that particular designation is not most relevant to the situation at hand. You want to know her name, not her family history. However, if my wife is at her mother’s workplace and is introduced by the term “Lisa’s daughter,” she has now been put in context in a very natural way. Her presence is explained by the fact that she is related to Lisa. Even though “Kate” and “Lisa’s daughter” are terms that designate the same human being, each highlights a different aspect of who she is—aspects that are more appropriate in some contexts than others.

The term “heart” is the proper term to use when talking about sanctification or moral change, as “heart” is the term that speaks to our inner person’s moral condition.[10] Sanctification is putting to death sinful tendencies and growing in righteousness. As such, change is placed right within the wheelhouse of the heart. As Anthony Hoekema points out,

> *The term soul, though it stands for the subject of all of man’s mental and spiritual activities, is not the best one to use [regarding man’s morality], since moral qualities are not attributed to the soul but to the heart. Man is said in Scripture to have a good heart or an evil heart, but not a good or evil soul.*[11]

The reason we speak about “heart change” is because the Bible views “heart” as the most encompassing term for how you and I function in life.[12] The heart is where our moral orientation lies. Our hearts are drawn toward the beauty and truthfulness of God, or they are repulsed by his holiness. The heart is also the source of the operations that constitute living. The heart is where our thinking, our desiring, and our choosing take place as we dynamically interact with ourselves, others, and our circumstances. The heart is the mind is the soul is the spirit, but when we come to talking about changing the whole inner person, it’s most proper to speak about the heart.

2 The Business That Never Closes

During my first year of seminary I worked the evening shift at a hotel to help pay the bills. During orientation, the property's general manager pointedly remarked, "This hotel opened seven years ago and we have been open every second since. Unlike most businesses, we never close." His goal in saying this was to impress upon the new hires that cleaning in a hotel cannot be relegated to when the doors are shut. Work and customers must exist side by side. And true to his words, I spent many nights cleaning common spaces, fixing balky internet connections, and running occupancy reports in the few scattered minutes between checking guests in and out.

"The business that never closes" is a fair description of us as people as well. From the moment an individual is born until he or she exhales for the final time, every person is dynamically interacting with the world around. We are not static, rocklike beings who simply sit and have waves wash over us to little immediate effect. Being loved makes us rejoice; being rejected makes us weep. A good meal brings delight and contentment. Watching a ball fall through a hoop makes half the audience cheer and the other bury their hands in their faces in despair. From the highest of heights to the most mundane moments, we are constantly perceiving, evaluating, and responding to the world around us. Even in sleep, we dream, and those dreams can occupy our thoughts and alter our moods in surprising ways. We never close.

Three Operations: Reasoning, Desiring, and Choosing

Theologians, philosophers, and psychologists typically identify three impulses, functions, or operations that consistently occur within our consciousness. Although these three functions have been categorized differently and gone by different names in different eras, they can more or less be identified as *reasoning*, *desiring*, and *choosing*.[13]

We can see these three processes at work the very moment we wake up. The second sleep ends and consciousness begins, our reason is at work. We perceive that we are no longer asleep but are awake. Thoughts begin their march, ranging from a hazy "Already?" to an enthusiastic "Yes! The day is here!"

None of these thoughts is the product of pure rationality, however. They are all blended with desires, which also immediately arise as soon as we perceive that wakefulness has begun. "Already?" is not a mere commentary on the earliness of the hour, but is wrapped with discouragement, disappointment, or frustration. "Yes! The day is here!" is indistinguishable from the excitement, joy, and invigoration that fuels the enthusiasm.

Our wills are also woven through our first experiences of the day. We may choose to indulge ourselves in grousing and complaining, or buckle under the pressures of the coming day by crawling back under the covers. On the other end of the spectrum, we may eagerly choose to leap out of bed and start the day—usually because there is some highly anticipated event.

These three processes operate within us every moment of every day. None can happen independent from the others, as reason, desires, and choosing are inextricably bound together. Every moment of every day we are thinking, desiring, and choosing beings. We are the business that never closes.

The Heart Is the Source of Reasoning, Desiring, and Choosing

Reasoning, desiring, and choosing (or willing) have been often portrayed as uneasy neighbors, locked in a kind of tug-of-war over who will direct the person. Much ancient Greek philosophy and medieval theology assumed that maturity came through taming one's unruly passions and desires by reason. In our day and age, we are rather oppositely urged to "follow your heart" (with "heart" being equated to one's desires). Culture assumes that our desires and emotions, more than our reason, represent our true selves. Still other traditions such as behaviorism place primary emphasis on our choices and habits.

Each of these approaches pictures the inner person as being subdivided into different pieces, with each piece being responsible for a different task. Our reason reasons, but it doesn't desire. Our affections love and yearn, but they do not think. Our will chooses, but it doesn't think or desire.

But this isn't how the Bible portrays our inner person. Throughout the Scriptures, our reasoning, desiring, and choosing are all described as processes of the heart. Consider how often the Bible explicitly roots our reasoning, our desiring, and our choosing in our hearts:

Reasoning

- "The LORD saw that the wickedness of man was great in the earth, and that every intention of the *thoughts of his heart* was only evil continually" (Gen. 6:5 ESV).[14]
- "Their eyes bulge out from fatness; the *imaginations of their hearts* run wild" (Ps. 73:7).
- "Perceiving their thoughts, Jesus said, 'Why are you *thinking evil things* in your hearts?'" (Matt. 9:4).
- "For *from the heart come evil thoughts*, murders, adulteries, sexual immoralities, thefts, false testimonies, slander" (Matt. 15:19).
- "For the word of God is living and effective and sharper than any double-edged sword, penetrating as far as the separation of soul and spirit, joints and marrow. It is able to judge the *thoughts* and intentions *of the heart*" (Heb. 4:12).
- "He has done a mighty deed with his arm; he has scattered the proud because of the *thoughts of their hearts*" (Luke 1:51).

Desiring

- "May he give you what your *heart desires* and fulfill your whole purpose" (Ps. 20:4).
- "You have given him his *heart's desire* and have not denied the request of his lips" (Ps. 21:2).
- "Because the sentence against an evil act is not carried out quickly, the *heart of the people is filled with the desire* to commit evil" (Eccl. 8:11).
- "Therefore God delivered them over in the *desires of their hearts* to sexual impurity, so that their bodies were degraded among themselves" (Rom. 1:24).
- "Brothers and sisters, my *heart's desire* and prayer to God concerning them is for their salvation" (Rom. 10:1).

Choosing (or Willing)

- "But you were not like my servant David, who kept my commands and *followed me with all his heart, doing only* what is right in my sight" (1 Kings 14:8).
- "It was *in my heart to build a house* as a resting place for the ark of the Lord's covenant and as a footstool for our God" (1 Chron. 28:2).
- "Give my son Solomon *an undivided heart to keep and to carry out* all your commands, your decrees, and your statutes, and to build the building for which I have made provision" (1 Chron. 29:19).
- "For from within, *out of people's hearts*, come evil thoughts, sexual immoralities, thefts, murders ..." (Mark 7:21).
- "A good person *produces good* out of the good stored up *in his heart*. An evil person *produces evil* out of the evil stored up *in his heart*, for *his mouth speaks from the overflow of the heart*" (Luke 6:45).

Each of these passages (and there are many more) follows a consistent pattern. The heart is the source or location of our reasoning, desiring, and choosing/willing. The *heart* reasons and thinks, the *heart* desires and loves, the *heart* chooses and wills.

The Union of All Three Processes

Let's draw the final strokes on our map of the inner person. We have already seen that reasoning, desiring, and choosing are products of our hearts. Now we must understand that all three of these processes are interwoven with one another. There is no such thing as pure reason, thoughtless desire, or desireless willing. The heart does not first reason, then switch over to desiring, then end with willing/choosing. All three processes are constantly happening at the same time.

Theologian Anthony Hoekema sought to explain how our hearts operate in this way by describing coming across a tree on a walk:

> *The perception of a tree is not a simple, but a complex process; it involves much more than a mere functioning of "the intellect." . . . Willing enters into it, since there must have been some kind of voluntary decision to fix one's attention to the tree. And feeling enters into it, since . . . [there] is always some dim consciousness of either pleasure or displeasure at the perception of a tree . . . . If, for example, the tree is seen as an object worthy of admiration for its own sake, it will excite pleasure; if, however, that same tree be perceived as an obstacle which interferes with a clear view of a beautiful landscape beyond it, the perception of the tree will be accompanied by pronounced displeasure.*[15]

Recognizing that all three processes are interrelated products of the heart keeps us from aiming at the wrong thing in helping people change. Consider for instance a problem where your car is operating sluggishly and tops out at 50 mph. You take it in to the mechanic and it's quickly established that the horsepower produced by the engine is lagging far behind what it ought to be. If your mechanic comes to you and informs you that he's going to need to replace your horsepower, it's time to find a new mechanic. The mechanic might need to change spark plugs, refresh an air filter, or overhaul the engine. But a mechanic will never replace the horsepower because horsepower isn't a "thing." It's a force produced by the engine.

In the same way, thinking, desiring, and choosing are *operations* of the heart, but are not entities in themselves. The heart produces thought, the heart produces desires, and the heart produces choices. But reasoning, desiring, and choosing/willing are all processes or functions or operations, not actual things inside of us. And like the engine, change must be targeted at the "thing" that is defective—namely, the heart. Any approach to change that places primary emphasis on only one impulse will ultimately stop short because it fails to purify the deepest reservoirs of who we are.[16]

The Heart: Orientation

As soon as the heart gets involved in our processes of reasoning, desiring, and choosing/willing, we have another factor that we must consider. The Bible describes the heart as having an orientation—it treasures righteousness or it treasures unrighteousness. Our hearts are not blank slates, but rather are deeply committed one way or the other.

Beneath all the uniqueness that God has bestowed upon each of his individual image bearers, human beings may be sorted into two categories based upon the orientation of their hearts. Speaking through the prophet Hosea, God calls the two groups "my people" and "not my people" *(Hos. 2:23)*. Those who follow Jesus' voice are his sheep, and those who do not are goats *(Matt. 25:31–33)*. When pictured as a garden, people are "wheat" or they are "weeds" *(Matt. 13:24–30)*. Indeed, the story of the whole Bible can be understood as the unfolding conflict between the "seed of the serpent" and the "seed of the woman" *(cf. Gen. 3:15)*.

One way Scripture consistently distinguishes between these two kinds of people on earth is by the way it describes their hearts. Behind the metaphors of wheat and weeds or sheep and goats lie two very different orientations of heart.

Orientation #1: Unrighteousness

The first heart orientation explicitly mentioned in the Bible is that of unrighteousness. The Lord looked down from heaven upon his image bearers in the time of Noah and was disturbed by what he saw: "The LORD saw that the wickedness of man was great in the earth, and that every intention of the thoughts of his heart was only evil continually" *(Gen. 6:5 ESV)*. The moral stench of humankind drove God to fill the earth with water, erasing his living creation except for the small population that clung to the ark. The flood waters cleansed the earth of wicked humanity; however, they did not change people's basic nature. The Lord's own promise not to flood the earth again clearly says so: "I will never again curse the ground because of human beings, even though the inclination of the human heart is evil from youth onward. And I will never again strike down every living thing as I have done" *(Gen. 8:21)*.

The remaining 1,181 chapters of the Bible use every possible hue to further describe this evil, unrighteous orientation of the heart. Pharaoh's rejection of the Lord and cruelties toward God's covenant people stem from a hard heart *(e.g., Ex. 4:21; 7:3, 13, 22)*. Sihon, king of Heshbon, similarly opposes the Israelites because his heart is "obstinate" *(Deut. 2:30)*. The Psalms are particularly expansive in their descriptions of a negative moral orientation of heart: the heart can be deceptive *(Ps. 12:2)*, full of malice *(28:3)*, unjust *(58:2)*, malicious *(66:18)*, disloyal *(78:8)*, insincere *(78:37)*, stubborn *(81:12)*, straying *(95:10)*, arrogant *(101:5)*, insensitive *(119:70)*, and, above all, evil *(41:6; 140:2; 141:4)*.

Proverbs continues the pattern of the Psalms, with wise King Solomon pleading with his son to avoid having an evil and perverse heart *(Prov. 6:14)*. Such a heart plots wicked schemes *(6:18)*, is full of sexual lust *(6:25)*, is wicked *(10:20)*, deceitful *(12:20)*, foolish *(12:23; 15:7)*, and proud *(16:5; 18:12)*, rages against the Lord *(19:3)*, and is arrogant *(21:4)*, violent *(24:2)*, glad when an enemy stumbles *(24:17)*, detestable *(26:25)*, hardened *(28:14)*, and, once again, evil *(26:23)*.

The New Testament carries on the theme of the heart having an unrighteous orientation. The heart is described as full of sexual lust *(Matt. 5:28; Rom. 1:24)*, callous *(Matt. 13:15; Acts 28:27)*, far from God *(Matt. 15:8)*, defiled *(Matt. 15:18)*, hardened *(Matt. 19:8; Mark 8:17; 16:14; Rom. 2:5; Eph. 4:18;*

Heb. 3:8, 15; 4:7), unbelieving *(Mark 16:14)*, proud *(Luke 1:51)*, lying *(Acts 5:4)*, uncircumcised *(Acts 7:51)*, not right before God *(Acts 8:21)*, senseless *(Rom. 1:21)*, unrepentant *(Rom. 2:5)*, straying *(Heb. 3:10)*, unbelieving *(Heb. 3:12)*, greedy *(2 Peter 2:14)*, and evil *(Matt. 9:4; 12:34; 15:19; Luke 6:45)*.

Worst of all, having an evil heart is the default state of every descendant of Adam who has walked the earth outside of the God-man, Jesus Christ. We are those of whom the Scriptures say that "the intention of man's heart is evil from his youth" *(Gen. 8:21 ESV)*.

Orientation #2: Righteousness

Although every child of Adam and Eve is born with a corrupt heart, the Bible does not describe our state as inflexibly evil. The human heart can be renewed through God's grace.

The Old Testament is full of positive descriptions of people's hearts. This righteous orientation is often described in reference to the person's relationship to the Lord. A righteous heart seeks the Lord *(Deut. 4:29; 1 Chron. 16:10; 22:19; 2 Chron. 11:16; 15:12; 19:3; 22:9; 30:19)*, loves the Lord *(Deut. 6:5; 11:13; 13:3; 30:6, 10)*, receives the word of the Lord *(1 Kings 3:9)*, stores up the word of the Lord *(Deut. 6:6; 11:18; 30:14; 32:46)*, worships the Lord *(Deut. 10:12; 11:13; 1 Sam. 12:24; 2 Chron. 29:31)*, faithfully obeys the Lord *(Deut. 26:16; 30:2; Josh. 22:5; 1 Kings 2:4; 8:23; 9:4; 2 Kings 23:3; 1 Chron. 29:19; 2 Chron. 34:31)*, follows the Lord *(2 Chron. 34:31)*, rejoices in the Lord *(1 Sam. 2:1; 1 Kings 8:66; 2 Chron. 7:10)*, covenants with the Lord *(2 Chron. 29:10; 34:31)*, and serves the Lord *(Deut. 28:47; Josh. 22:5; 2 Kings 23:25)*.

The heart is also frequently described as being connected directly to righteous functioning. The heart is generous *(Ex. 35:5, 22, 29)*, righteously reasons *(Josh. 23:14; 1 Kings 3:12; Job 38:36)*, is wise *(1 Kings 3:12; 10:24; Job 38:36)*, is tender to conviction *(2 Kings 22:19; 2 Chron. 34:27)*, is morally upright *(1 Chron. 29:17)*, and is faithful *(Neh. 9:8)*.

The book of Psalms is especially rich in its description of the heart's righteous capacities. This is unsurprising given how that book more than any other describes the range of feelings that we experience as human beings. Throughout the Psalms, the heart is full of joy *(Ps. 4:7)*, is thankful *(9:1; 138:1)*, and rejoices in God's deliverance *(13:5; 28:7)*. It acknowledges truth *(15:2)*, delights in God's presence *(16:9)*, is upright and free from evil *(7:10; 11:2; 17:3; 24:4; 26:1–2; 32:11; 36:10; 64:10; 73:1, 13; 94:15; 97:11; 119:7, 80)*, rejoices at God's law and character *(19:8; 33:21)*, seeks the Lord *(27:8; 105:3; 119:2, 10, 58; 125:4)*, is full of courage and confidence *(27:14; 108:1; 112:7–8)*, trusts in the Lord *(28:7)*, treasures God's instruction *(37:31; 119:11, 70, 111)*, is righteous *(40:10)*, faithfully follows God *(44:18; 119:34)*, is full of wisdom *(49:3; 90:12)*, is humble *(51:17; 131:1)*, is full of praise to the Lord *(86:12; 111:1)*, has integrity *(101:2)*, obeys the Lord *(119:34, 69)*, and calls out to the Lord *(119:149)*.

The focus on wisdom in the book of Proverbs provides another view of the righteous heart. A Godward-oriented heart righteously reasons *(Prov. 2:2)*, is wise *(2:10; 11:29; 14:30, 33; 16:21, 23; 23:15)*, holds on to the words of other wise people *(3:1; 4:4, 20–21; 6:20–21; 7:2–3; 23:26)*, is loyal and faithful *(3:3)*, trusts in the Lord *(3:5)*, listens to instruction *(10:8)*, is full of peace *(14:30)*, is full of joy *(15:13, 15, 30; 17:22; 27:11)*, and is pure *(22:11)*.

The New Testament continues the pattern of referring to the heart as capable of righteousness. In the Gospels we see that those who are "pure in heart" are blessed because they will see God *(Matt. 5:8)*. Jesus centers the law on loving the Lord with all your heart *(Matt. 22:37; Mark 12:30, 33; Luke 10:27)*, and refers to the heart as a storehouse of good *(Luke 6:45)*. The heart may also be good and honest, and thus receive the sown seed *(Luke 8:15)*. The hearts of Jesus' listeners "burn[ed]" within them, stirred by his revelation of himself as the Messiah *(Luke 24:32)*. Jesus promises that at his resurrection his followers' "heart[s] will rejoice" *(John 16:22 NASB)*.

The remainder of the New Testament particularly focuses on describing moral virtues of the heart. The heart possesses joy *(Acts 2:46; 14:17)*, sincerity *(Acts 2:46; Eph. 6:5)*, unity *(Acts 4:32; Col. 2:2)*, devotion to the Lord *(Acts 11:23)*, purity *(Acts 15:9; 1 Tim. 1:5; 2 Tim. 2:22; Heb. 10:22; 1 Peter 1:22)*, and obedience *(Rom. 6:17; Eph. 6:6)*. It sorrows over unbelief and sin *(Rom. 9:2; 2 Cor. 2:4)*, believes in the Lord *(Rom. 10:9–10)*, and is responsive to the Lord's work *(2 Cor. 4:6; Eph. 1:18)*, transformed by the Lord *(2 Cor. 3:3)*, worshipful *(Eph. 5:19)*, peaceful *(Phil. 4:7; Col. 3:15)*, grateful *(Col. 3:16)*, holy *(1 Thess. 3:13)*, responsive to God's love and Christ's endurance *(2 Thess. 3:5)*, written upon with God's law *(Heb. 8:10, 16)*, established by grace *(Heb. 13:9)*, and gentle *(1 Peter 3:4)*. Lastly, the heart is also the residence of the Spirit of Christ, the down payment of our future glory *(2 Cor. 1:22; Gal. 4:6; Eph. 3:17)*.

It's essential to see in this much detail how the Bible describes our inner person. Scripture is not shy about assigning moral qualities to the core of who we are. The human heart may be oriented toward unrighteousness or it may be oriented toward righteousness. Chapter 4 will explore how the heart can change orientation, but for now the most important thing to recognize is that the Bible describes some people as having a heart that is pointed toward righteousness and others as having a heart pointed toward unrighteousness.

The Orientation of the Heart Determines the Moral Quality of Its Operations

To sum up what we've seen thus far in this chapter, we have detailed two levels to the heart. First, the heart operates dynamically. Every moment of our consciousness is filled with willing, thinking, reasoning, desiring, choosing, loving, and all the other words that we use to describe the rich web of impulses that constitute our inner experience. Second, our hearts are not morally neutral, but rather are oriented either toward or away from righteousness or unrighteousness.

Placing these two realities on top of each other allows us to see something critical: the orientation of our hearts dictates the morality of our reasoning, desiring, and willing. In other words, unrighteous thoughts, desires, and choices come from an unrighteous heart, while righteous thoughts, desires, and choices come from a righteous heart. The Bible portrays the closest connection possible between the orientation of our hearts and the operation of our hearts, as Jesus famously teaches: "You'll recognize them by their fruit .... Every good tree produces good fruit, but a bad tree produces bad fruit. A good tree can't produce bad fruit; neither can a bad tree produce good fruit" *(Matt. 7:16–18)*. This is why attempts to change must be focused on the heart. Trying to change thoughts from unrighteous to righteous without changing the heart is like trying to purify water downstream of a toxic waste dump. Our thoughts and reason, desires and emotions, and will and choices are derivative of our hearts.

The products of the human heart are naturally colored by the orientation of the heart. The wickedness that emerges from the heart in a person's thoughts, desires, and choices is produced by the direction in which that person's heart points. Like water from a contaminated well, the thoughts, desires, and actions that emerge from the heart are poisoned because the heart itself is poisoned. And righteous thoughts, desires, and actions are like a clean, crisp glass of water coming from a clean aquifer. A beautiful, regenerated heart will produce righteous deeds because the heart is now righteous. The fruit of the Spirit naturally blossoms in the heart of a believer because the heart has been changed into a fountain of love, joy, peace, patience, kindness, goodness, gentleness, faithfulness, and self-control.

Jesus' short parable about fruit trees is not meant to be the only word on the interplay between the heart's orientation and operation. Those who are unrighteous can do works that are good for humanity. Those of us whose hearts have been transformed still struggle with sin, as we wrestle with the clinging remains of our sin nature that will not be cast aside fully until death. However, the overall point of Jesus' teaching is unmistakable. The orientation of the heart determines the moral quality of its operations. A righteous heart produces righteous thoughts, desires, and choices. An unrighteous heart produces unrighteous thoughts, desires, and choices.

Part II

Understanding Different Kinds of Change

3 Yes, Unbelievers Can Really Change

My four-year old's world destabilized the day he discovered that tornadoes are more than just an idea. He had abstractly known about tornadoes for a while, but an hour spent with Mommy and brother barricaded inside our master bathroom while a twister tore through the downtown of our city brought the idea sharply into his mind in a way he'd never considered.

That hour changed him. The idea of a lurching, writhing cloud that could suck up cars and people and snap trees suddenly made nature seem redder in tooth and claw than he had imagined possible. Gone was our happy-go-lucky little tiger, replaced by a child who would sprint from the van to the house, then stand shaking by the front door while we unbuckled his brother. In his mind, tornadoes could strike at any minute, even if it was a sunny day without a cloud in the sky.

Eventually he and I started devoting a little time to intentionally working on his fear of tornadoes. We sat on the front step of our home for a few minutes at the close of the day, just talking. At first the poor little guy was on the brink of tears, casting worried glances at the sky every few seconds. Over time he came to accept two foundational truths which convinced him that playing outside could be fun again and wasn't an exercise in standing before the yawning jaws of death. First, tornadoes do not emerge suddenly from the sky, but there are ways adults can tell if they're coming. Two, you only have to be scared when Mommy and Daddy are scared.

Who Can Experience Change?

My son's brief adventure with tornadoes illustrates a very important reality. Every single human being is not only capable of change, but actually experiences change day by day. The event of hiding in the bathroom with Mommy and brother gave rise to new thoughts, new desires, and new choices within my son's life. He now felt fear because he had grown in knowledge, namely, that a particular kind of wind could hurt him. His strong desires for safety manifested themselves in new choices. Instead of running toward the backyard full of delight, he sprinted for the indoors, which he perceived to be a sanctuary of safety. My conversations with him likewise created new realities that did not exist before we had them. His thoughts were focused in a different direction as we taught him to key his fears off of Mommy and Daddy rather than his perception of the world. He rediscovered delight in the outdoors in light of these new truths. And he chose to abandon his indoor sanctuary for the rekindled joy of digging in the mud and bouncing on the trampoline.

Sometimes the idea is carelessly thrown around in Christian circles that "only Christians can experience *real* change." I think I understand what is meant by that phrase, but the problem is that it is patently false. One of the core differentiating factors between God and human beings is that he is immutable and we are mutable. We change; he does not.[17] We all, like my son, experience change through the rising and falling of all kinds of things within us throughout our day-to-day experience. Happiness wells up as a favored song plays on the radio. A phone call may create grief, or a reckless driver, anger. All of these experiences involve the creation of very real thoughts, desires, and choices that did not exist prior to each event. Such changes are not fake or a hazy mirage.

Another idea that sometimes rears its head is that "only Christians can experience *lasting* change." This line of thought acknowledges that every human being changes, but claims that only those who have experienced regeneration are capable of changing in a way that endures. Once again, this statement runs aground on the reef of simple observation. Frat boys pick themselves up off the alcohol-saturated ground and become responsible, productive members of society with steady jobs and steady families. Couples that toed right up to the edge of the cliff of divorce step back and learn to live in harmony with each other. Many of those walking on this planet bear physical scars from a suicide attempt that was never repeated because despair gave way to hope. We all know individuals who fall into these and other categories of significant and positive change, yet who have experienced this change without becoming Christians. Real, lasting change has occurred independent of their hearts being transformed by the Holy Spirit.

While the idea that only Christians can experience real or lasting change is certainly incorrect, such comments are attempting to capture a very important distinction. Not all change is created equal and not all change that looks similar flows from the same headwater. Change comes in a variety of forms, with a variety of motivations, and has a variety of effects.[18] In order to understand how this is the case, we must look at how the heart's orientation toward righteousness or unrighteousness dictates the kind of change that a person can experience.

The Unbelieving Heart Is Dead and Expresses Itself in Rebellion

All people begin life with a default state of rejecting God. This rejection is manifested in many different ways and the Bible uses a cornucopia of words, metaphors, and concepts to provide texture and warmth to its picture of how human beings experience and express their rejection of God. Those who have turned away from their Creator are described in terms of blindness *(Matt. 23:16)*, prostitution (Ezek. 16:1–63), and whitewashed tombs *(Matt. 23:27)*. Two of the most common pictures God provides for us are death and rebellion. To use the language from Part I of this book, deadness speaks to the heart's *orientation*, while rebellion speaks to its *operations* or functions. Deadness and rebellion are traveling companions, as the heart's orientation and operations are inseparably wound together.

Deadness

The Scriptures are bursting with passages that lay forth the deadness inherent to the descendants of Adam. We all lie in a spiritual graveyard, our hearts entirely corrupt and lifeless.

- "And you were dead in your trespasses and sins in which you previously walked according to the ways of this world" *(Eph. 2:1–2)*.
- "Get up, sleeper, and rise up from the dead, and Christ will shine on you" *(Eph. 5:14)*.
- "You were dead in trespasses and in the uncircumcision of your flesh" *(Col. 2:13)*.
- "She who is self-indulgent is dead even while she lives" *(1 Tim. 5:6)*.
- "I know your works; you have a reputation for being alive, but you are dead" *(Rev. 3:1)*.

While none of these passages explicitly uses the term "heart," the "you" in view is clearly the inner person. When the Scriptures say a person is dead, it specifically means that person's heart is dead.[19]

Rebellion

The deadness of an unbeliever's heart categorically rules out any ability for him or her to think, desire, or choose righteously. Hebrews 11:6 makes this inability clear: "Without faith it is impossible to please God." Faith is a product of a heart that has been made alive by the Holy Spirit, and dead hearts cannot possess faith without first experiencing regeneration. Because dead hearts can express themselves only in a manner consistent with their deadness, unbelievers think dead thoughts, desire deathly things, and make death-infused choices. The Bible gives us a sampling of the kinds of rebellion that emerge from dead hearts:

- "The Lord saw that the wickedness of man was great in the earth, and that every intention of the thoughts of his heart was only evil continually" (Gen. 6:5 ESV).
- "They lie to one another; they speak with flattering lips and deceptive hearts" (Ps. 12:2).
- "You did more evil than your ancestors. Look, each one of you was following the stubbornness of his evil heart, not obeying me" (Jer. 16:12).

- "But what comes out of the mouth comes from the heart, and this defiles a person. For from the heart come evil thoughts, murders, adulteries, sexual immoralities, thefts, false testimonies, slander" (Matt. 15:18–19).
- "You stiff-necked people with uncircumcised hearts and ears! You are always resisting the Holy Spirit" (Acts 7:51).
- "They have eyes full of adultery that never stop looking for sin. They seduce unstable people and have hearts trained in greed" (2 Peter 2:14).

Every one of these passages links the rebellious thoughts, desires, and choices made by human beings to the moral deadness of their hearts. An unbeliever's expressed unrighteousness is not a product of happenstance or the result of ignorant misdirection. Those who are of the flesh *cannot* please God, which means that every thought, desire, and choice made by an unbeliever is an exploration of what deadness looks like when expressed in human life.[20]

Civic Righteousness

We must be careful at this juncture, lest we tumble off a path that Scripture carefully carves through the cliffs of error. We have affirmed that every thought, desire, and choice that emerges from an unbelieving heart is unrighteous because without faith it is impossible to please God. This does not mean, however, that every possible thought, desire, and choice available to the unbeliever is equally unrighteous. An unbeliever who walks away from the ravages of substance abuse and into sobriety has experienced good and positive change. His new manner of life is better for him and better for those who love him. Yet, according to God's testimony, that change did not please God because it was not sourced from and accompanied by faith.

Theologians from times past are able to lend us a helping hand in figuring out this rather complex dance. The Westminster Confession of Faith devotes a section to the nature of good works done by unbelievers:

> *Although the works done by unregenerate men may in themselves be things which God commands and things which*

> *are useful to themselves and others, yet—because they do not come from a heart purified by faith, are not done in a right manner according to the Word, and are not done for the right purpose, which is to glorify God—they are therefore sinful, and cannot please God or make one suitable to receive his grace. Yet, neglecting them is even more sinful and displeasing to God.*[21]

This section of the confession clearly affirms the inability of unbelievers to please God and live righteously. But it adds two crucial points to our discussion. First, unbelievers are able to do things that God commands. Second, even though doing the things God commands is still ultimately an expression of rebellion given their dead hearts, not doing the things God has commanded is an even greater expression of rebellion. An unbeliever who restores a lost little girl to her parents in a crowded grocery store has been compassionate, and God commands compassion. However, this action is not morally laudable before God because it was not driven by faith in God and a desire to please him. Nevertheless, it would be a far greater expression of unrighteousness for the unbeliever to quash all inklings of compassion and callously walk past the weeping little girl.

We are all grateful for (and many of us are beneficiaries of) unbelievers who extend kindness to a lost child. Theologians often call the kind of righteousness unbelievers can express "civic righteousness."[22] Civic righteousness is good for individuals and for society. Obeying God's commands (such as in kindness, selflessness, and love) naturally leads to a more harmonious society. We are grateful for unbelievers who have worked to eradicate crippling diseases, fund scholarships for gifted yet financially challenged students, and fight to bring injustice to an end. However, these works are simultaneously good for humanity and of no benefit before God. Civic righteousness lies firmly within the reach of unbelievers, even as true moral righteousness eludes them because of the deadness of their hearts.

A Spectrum from Hitler to Nana

The category of civic righteousness is an important one for our current study on change. All dead hearts do not operate with the same level of wickedness. If we can imagine a spectrum of unrighteousness, on the one side we have a rogues' gallery of wicked men and women whose names are synonymous with cruelty: Nero, Vlad the Impaler, Hitler, Stalin, Mao, Sanger. These individuals are memorable for their expressions of unrighteousness that scandalize the consciences even of unbelievers. They stand out not because of their wicked hearts, but because of just how wicked their heart expressions are in contrast with the hearts of other unbelievers. At the other end of the spectrum, we have kindly grandmothers who feed the entire block with pies made from scratch, yet are entirely unconverted.

If we are to rightly understand the different kinds of change people may experience, we must recognize that any point on the spectrum from Hitler to Grandma is available to any unbeliever. An unbeliever's dead and rebellious heart may manifest itself through unspeakable cruelty or by kind acts that are poisoned by the lack of faith underneath. In other words, the *operations* of the heart may be changed without there being a prior change in the *orientation* of the heart.

Consider the case of an unbelieving father whose strictness and harshness toward his teenage son has driven a wedge between the two of them. Through the encouragement of his wife and others the father comes to recognize that the relational gulf is primarily a result of his own attitudes and actions. The father dedicates himself to changing the way he expresses himself toward his son, seeking to encourage rather than to prod.

Real change has occurred within this father. He thinks differently, as he has come to believe that encouragement rather than brusqueness is the best way to relate to his son. His desire for control has been superseded by a desire to have a positive relationship with his son that endures beyond his soon-arriving eighteenth birthday. He now chooses to express himself in ways that are clearly encouraging and build up rather than through a tough-love gruffness. The father has genuinely changed in the operations or expressions of his heart. He has different thoughts, desires, and choices that are being observably expressed in time and space.

However, no regeneration, no actual change in the orientation of the father's heart, is necessary for him to change in these ways. A person does not need to be reconciled to the

Father, Son, and Holy Spirit in order to love his own son and speak affectionately to him.[23] The operations of the father's heart have shifted dramatically, but this shift can occur without God's saving grace working on his heart because gruffness and encouragement are both possible expressions of a dead and rebellious heart.

This is not to say that unbelievers may change the operations of their hearts with whiplash-inducing rapidity. Our patterns of living are not unmoored from the ways we habitually express our hearts. A man who has spent his whole life cruelly mocking his family is unlikely to decide while waking up one morning to become tender in his interactions with his children. We all grow accustomed to the habitual ways in which our hearts operate, which are often very difficult to break.[24] However, should such a man demonstrate change, it does not automatically mean that God has transformed his heart, as cruelty and kindness are both possible expressions of a dead and rebellious heart.

Biblical Case Study: King Josiah's Reforms

The biblical account of King Josiah's reforms provides an excellent illustration of how human beings may change in their hearts' expressions without experiencing a change in their hearts' orientation (2 Kings 22–23; 2 Chron. 34–35). Josiah ascended to the throne of Judah long after its glory had faded. Gone were the days of David and Solomon when the nations streamed in to see Israel's riches and power. Josiah's kingdom comprised only two small tribes, whose hearts had been corrupted by a long succession of kings who rejected the living God. Josiah, however, was one of the handful of rulers who loved the Lord and desired to uphold the Mosaic law.

The extent of Josiah's reforms is quite incredible, told in painstaking detail. At his orders:

- The temple is emptied of articles made for Baal, Asherah, and the stars of the sky.
- The idolatrous priests who worship Baal, Asherah, and the sun, moon, and constellations are removed from the high places.
- The high places are defiled from Geba to Beer-sheba (the

northern tip to the southern tip of the populated portion of Judah—the equivalent of saying "from New York to San Diego").

- The place of human sacrifice to Molech at Topheth is defiled.
- The chariots of the sun are destroyed.
- The altars on top of the king's residence are ripped apart.
- The unauthorized altars in the courtyards of the temple are destroyed.
- The altars to Chemosh, Milcom, and Ashtoreth are defiled.
- Jeroboam's altar for Israel rivaling the one in the temple in Jerusalem is destroyed.
- The shrines throughout Samaria are also torn down and their priests are slaughtered.
- The mediums and spiritists are eradicated.
- The household idols and images are banished.

Josiah does not stop at the mere destruction of evil, however, but leads the people of Judah in a covenant renewal service. The king and the people vow to be reconciled to the Lord and live according to his good commands:

> *Next, the king stood by the pillar and made a covenant in the LORD's presence to follow the LORD and to keep his commands, his decrees, and his statutes with all his heart and with all his soul in order to carry out the words of this covenant that were written in this book; all the people agreed to the covenant.*
>
> *(2 Kings 23:3)*

The priests begin again their sacrifices to the Lord, sacrifices that had before been compromised by the presence of despicable idols crowding around the most holy places. A renewed covenant and restored sacrifices led to a reconvened Passover celebration. While the diminished Judah could not rival David and Solomon's kingdom for splendor, its remembrance of the Passover excelled all prior Passovers in the Promised Land. The author of 2 Kings recollects that "no such Passover had ever been observed from the time of the judges who judged Israel through the entire time of the kings of Israel and Judah" (2 Kings 23:22).

Our survey of this biblical account demonstrates that *real* change has occurred within the nation of Judah during Josiah's reforms. The pagan priests who used to offer detestable sacrifices are now dead, their bones scattered in judgment. The idols of stone and timber before which the Judahites used to commit ritual prostitution and kill their children have been bludgeoned to pieces. The special blend of incense authorized for use only in the temple rises out of the holy places in worship to God.

Behind each of these actions lay changes in men and women's thoughts, desires, and choices. The people now reasoned and considered that it was better to follow their king in the worship of the Lord than in the worship of other gods. They desired God's blessing and so actively chose, moment by moment, to observe his law. The operations of their hearts changed under the guidance of Josiah, and in dramatic fashion.

Pretense

Things certainly appear to be going well in Judah. A righteous king sits on the throne, sacrifices are once again happening according to the Lord's instruction, and the people have promised to faithfully follow God's law. However, God offers his evaluation of the people of Judah through the prophet Jeremiah:

> *In the days of King Josiah the* Lord *asked me, "Have you seen what unfaithful Israel has done? She has ascended every high hill and gone under every green tree to prostitute herself there. I thought, 'After she has done all these things, she will return to me.' But she didn't return, and her treacherous sister Judah saw it. I observed that it was because unfaithful Israel had committed adultery that I had sent her away and had given her a certificate of divorce. Nevertheless, her treacherous sister Judah was not afraid but also went and prostituted herself. Indifferent to her prostitution, she defiled the land and committed adultery with stones and trees. Yet in spite of all*

> *this, her treacherous sister Judah didn't return to*
> *me with all her heart—only in pretense."*
> *This is the Lord's declaration.*
>
> (*Jer.* 3:6–10)

The Lord sees far deeper into the Israelites than any human being can. Behind all the new thoughts, desires, and choices he sees the condition of their hearts. What he sees leads him to speak words of judgment rather than praise.

Judah has not returned to the Lord with "all her heart," but only "in pretense." Such a description acknowledges that real change has taken place within the people of the country. After all, the word "pretense" assumes that something is different. The Lord recognizes that Josiah's reforms have changed the way in which the Judahites are worshipping; however, he also declares that none of these changes stems from a change of heart.[25] In other words, the operations of their hearts (thoughts, desires, choices) have changed, but the orientation of their hearts has not shifted away from death and rebellion toward life. The people are still violating the first commandment to not have any other gods before the Lord while engaging in his rituals. The people have simply caught a different breeze and are blowing with the wind toward the temple instead of the high places.

	Thoughts	**Desires**	**Choices**
Old	Appeasing Ashtoreth will bring blessings across every category of life	Love to self, manifested as a desire to perform sacrifices that appease Ashtoreth	Following the pattern of worship dictated by Ashtoreth
New	Appeasing Yahweh (the Lord) will bring blessings across every category of life	Love to self, manifested as a desire to perform sacrifices that appease Yahweh (the Lord)	Following the pattern of worship dictated by the law, including Passover, sacrifice, and "monotheism"

The table above highlights how the people of Judah can have new thoughts, desires, and choices, and yet not have experienced any regeneration of their hearts. Each of these new thoughts, desires, and choices is an expression of a dead, rebellious heart. One need not have a living relationship with the Lord to live out ritualistic worship of him, a fact we continue to see played out in our churches today.

What's Missing?

God does not leave us in the dark as to why he relegates his people's transformation to the dustbin of "pretense." Jeremiah records the Lord's reflection:

> *Return, unfaithful Israel.*
> *This is the LORD's declaration.*
> *I will not look on you with anger,*
> *for I am unfailing in my love.*
> *This is the LORD's declaration.*
> *I will not be angry forever.*
> *Only acknowledge your guilt—*
> *you have rebelled against the LORD your God.*
> *You have scattered your favors to strangers*
> *under every green tree*
> *and have not obeyed me.*
>
> . . .
>
> *Circumcise yourselves to the LORD;*
> *remove the foreskin of your hearts,*
> *men of Judah and residents of Jerusalem.*
>
> *(Jer. 3:11–13; 4:4)*

The change experienced by the people of Judah is mere pretense because it lacks repentance. They have not reckoned with the fact that their covenant unfaithfulness has left them mired in actual moral guilt before the Lord which cannot be taken away by swapping one form of worship for another. Many years prior, after violating God's covenant by abusing his kingly power through sexual abuse, murder, and cover-ups, King David reflected, "You do not want a sacrifice, or I would give it; you are not pleased with a burnt offering. The sacrifice pleasing to God is a broken spirit. You will not despise a broken and humbled heart, God" (Ps. 51:16–17). The people of Judah need their hearts to be circumcised, for their deadness and rebellion to be washed clean. Until that happens, the change they have experienced is merely change in the operation of their hearts. They have shuffled from one spot to another on the spectrum from Hitler to Nana. In the Lord's words, such change is not a sign of any true moral virtue, but mere pretense.

Love the Lord with All Your Heart

The tragic tale of Josiah and the people of Judah puts flesh and blood to the distinction between changes in the heart's expression and a change in heart orientation. The people of Judah were able to refrain from burning their children in the killing fields of Molech because dead hearts do not irrevocably express themselves through child murder. Replacing human blood with the sacrifice of bulls, lambs, and grain was a positive change within Judah—especially if you were an infant. However, these changes do not indicate a change in the orientation of the people's hearts. To recall the words of the Westminster Confession quoted earlier, "because [these offerings] do not come from a heart purified by faith, are not done in a right manner according to the Word, and are not done for the right purpose, which is to glorify God—they are therefore sinful, and cannot please God or make one suitable to receive his grace."

When a lawyer quizzed Jesus regarding the law's greatest command, Jesus centered his response on the inner man: "Love the Lord your God with all your heart, with all your soul, and with all your mind. This is the greatest and most important command" (Matt. 22:37–38). The point of the law was to cause a deep love for God to well up within the hearts of those whom he had chosen from among all the peoples of the earth. King Josiah manifested this kind of living faith in the Lord—"Before him there was no king like him who turned to the LORD with all his heart and with all his soul and with all his strength according to all the law of Moses, and no one like him arose after him" (2 Kings 23:25). What a contrast with the people. Josiah's subjects followed his reforms but not his heart. Although they changed in the operations of their hearts through new thoughts, desires, and choices, no change had happened within the core of their being. They did not love the Lord.

Operation Change and Helping People

The category of changes in a heart's expression helps us as we seek to care for people within our churches, ministries, families, and other contexts. It provides an explanation for the vexing question of why unbelievers can change for the better without the Spirit of God transforming their hearts. Such change is indeed real and may very well be lasting, but it is simply the shifting of deadness and rebellion from one expression to another. These changes often are good and healthful for the unbelievers themselves and for those around them, but they are not meritorious before God or indicative of hearts that have been brought from death to life.

Another facet of life that this category helps us make sense of is the general success of secular psychotherapy. Most major schools of thought within psychology have been heavily studied through empirical testing. Some of this testing has been driven by rivalry with other schools of thought, and some has been driven to legitimize the discipline of psychiatry as a whole.[26]

Regardless of the motivation for testing, many forms of therapy have been proven effective in helping the majority of patients, especially for troubles such as anxiety and depression.[27] Meeting with a secular counselor or psychologist has helped no small number of human beings work through the dark clouds of depression, paralyzing anxiety, and a whole host of other issues. As fellow human beings made in the image of God, we should be thankful for these positive changes. However, we must also recognize that these changes most often take place without any reference to the true and living God. Because such changes do not come from faith, and without faith it is impossible to please God, such changes are only in their heart's expression, rather than being any actual change of heart. Secular therapy may contribute toward civic righteousness, but it typically does not move the heart toward life. Until the deepest part of the person is brought to life through regeneration, none of these changes is of moral benefit before God.

4 Yes, Christians Change Differently

My wife and I both grew up on the central coast of California. This stretch of the state is rural, dotted by small coastal communities and even smaller towns scattered across the hot, dusty interior. I played baseball and she played softball on fields tucked in between oil pump jacks and scrub brush, with the green of the field being the only interruption in the dry, brown landscape.

We are now raising our own little family in South Carolina. The dusty landscape has been replaced by inescapable hues of green, driven by very different weather. We have weeks where the total precipitation exceeds our California hometown's yearly allotment of rainfall.

One routine we continue to struggle with is the need to actually check the weather rather than just glancing at the sky in the morning. In California, sun begets sun. Here, it's quite common to have a sunny morning be followed by a dark, rain-soaked afternoon.

Every thunderstorm that rolls across our new town comes in two stages. First, the weather changes as the temperature drops, the wind kicks up, and the sun is eclipsed from view. Then, the rain begins in earnest as clouds drop their water to be drunk up by the verdant forests.

A rolling afternoon thunderstorm provides a helpful picture of the change we will look at in this chapter. While the previous chapter detailed change that occurs only within the expressions of the heart, we move now to look at the kind of change that transforms the heart itself. Like a thunderstorm, heart change happens in two different yet intimately connected stages.

The First Change: Regeneration

Our last chapter established that the most defining truth about a non-Christian's heart is that it is spiritually dead. This spiritual deadness leaves true righteousness out of reach, as "without faith it is impossible to please God" (Heb. 11:6).

Our study in this chapter of genuine heart change must also start with the spiritually limp and lifeless heart. This is the default state of every person, but it is not an unalterable state. In one of the most glorious passages of the Bible, Paul emphatically declares, "You were dead in your trespasses and sins .... But God, who is rich in mercy, because of his great love that he had for us, made us alive with Christ even though we were dead in trespasses" (Eph. 2:1, 4–5). Because the Father loved us, he reached out and brought us to spiritual life.

God's gracious act to bring us out of spiritual death and into spiritual life is the first kind of heart change the Bible describes. The theological word that captures this event is "regeneration."

The Bible describes what happens when someone becomes a Christian in a variety of rich and multifaceted ways. For example, a person is "adopted," meaning that they have now become a member of God's family, giving them a place to belong and an inheritance. A person is "justified," as God declares them not guilty of their sins because Christ has paid their penalty. These terms (and many others) each give us a different window by which we may see the sum total of what happens when a person becomes a Christian. "Adoption" takes a familial look at the event of salvation, while "justification" speaks to the legal process. "Regeneration" is likewise part of what occurs at salvation, with a special focus on what's going on within the heart.

The actual word "regeneration" appears only once in most English translations, where Paul reminds Titus that God "saved us—not by works of righteousness that we had done, but according to his mercy—through the washing of regeneration and renewal by the Holy Spirit" (Titus 3:5). However, the concept of the heart being renewed or coming to life pervades the pages of Scripture.

The most famous passage that describes regeneration is a conversation between Jesus and Nicodemus. Jesus tells the befuddled member of the Sanhedrin that he must be "born again" in order to receive eternal life (John 3:3ff.). This concept is spoken of in different ways all through the New Testament.

Peter describes the church as comprising those who have "been born again—not of perishable seed but of imperishable—through the living and enduring word of God" (1 Peter 1:23). John earlier noted that human beings must be "born, not of natural descent, or of the will of the flesh, or of the will of man, but of God" (John 1:13). Paul reminded the ritual-trusting Galatian church that "both circumcision and uncircumcision mean nothing; what matters instead is a new creation" (Gal. 6:15). Elsewhere Paul reminded the Ephesians that they must "put on the new self, the one created according to God's likeness in righteousness and purity of the truth" (Eph. 4:24).[28] And although regeneration is not as prominently featured in the Old Testament, it certainly may be seen in the emphasis on the "circumcision of the heart" (Deut. 10:16; 30:6; Jer. 4:4).

"Regeneration" is thus a word used to denote a biblical concept spoken of in many ways—the heart coming alive under the hand of God as he graciously draws a rebellious sinner back to himself. Theologian Charles Hodge aptly describes regeneration as "the instantaneous change from spiritual death to spiritual life. Regeneration, therefore, is a spiritual resurrection; the beginning of a new life."[29] To use our categories from above, regeneration changes the orientation of our hearts. We were once rebellious toward God and goodness, but now we love his person and his instruction.

Think for a moment of flying on an airplane. There's a moment in every flight where the orientation changes. One moment you're at the cruising altitude of 38,000 feet. The plane is level, maintaining its course and speed. Then, even though you're a long ways off from your destination, a change occurs. The nose of the plane pitches down as the descent begins. The plane's orientation has gone from parallel to the ground to pointing downward. Its orientation has changed.

So it is within our hearts. Regeneration brings our hearts to life and changes our orientation. We were oriented toward death, but now we have life. We were oriented toward rebellious self-rule, but now we have humbled ourselves under the mighty hand of God. We were masters of our own fate, but now we cede control to our Lord.

Regeneration and Heart Operations

It's at this juncture that our study in chapters 1 and 2 of the nature of the heart and its operations becomes critically important for understanding change. If our hearts are subdivided into different compartments, where does regeneration primarily take place? Some theologians have understood our powers of reason to be the central part of our hearts; consequently regeneration is understood primarily as a restoration of the ability to think rightly.[30] Still others have described our affections or will as central.[31] Regeneration then primarily centers around changing our desires. Both approaches are highly problematic, shrinking the reach of regeneration by placing it primarily within one function. Growth in the Christian life becomes unbalanced as it must then be primarily intellectual or emotional.

Reformed theologian Louis Berkhof provides a better picture of how regeneration affects our inner person:

> *Regeneration is not . . . simply a change in one or more of the faculties of the soul, as, for instance, of the emotional life . . . or of the intellect. It affects the heart . . . that is, the central and all-controlling organ of the soul, out of which are the issues of life. This means that it affects human nature as a whole.*[32]

Regeneration affects the heart itself directly, and transformed thoughts, desires, and choices emerge from that transformed heart. Regeneration opens up our hearts to be able to express themselves in ways never before possible because of the limiting effect of spiritual deadness. Petrus van Mastricht described regeneration as the moment when a human being is "restored by God to . . . lost goodness."[33] Because the heart's orientation itself has changed, the heart may now operate in goodness. God-glorifying patterns of thought, loves and desires, and choices are now possible because the heart itself has new life pumping through its veins.

Unlike the change we looked at in the previous chapter, this change in the orientation of the heart through regeneration is not a product of human effort. No person will ever muster up the ability to change their own heart because they do not naturally desire to do so. Berkhof describes regeneration as "that act of God by which the principle of the new life is implanted in man, and the governing disposition of the soul is made holy."[34] In Paul's words, regeneration "does not depend on human will or effort but on God who shows mercy" (Rom. 9:16). Regeneration by definition is an *act of God*, not a result of our own will.

A change in the heart's orientation is thus an entirely different species from changes in its expression or operations. This change comes from God, not from our own self-determination. It's nothing less than life bursting forth where formerly all was death.

A New Nature, but Plenty of Trouble

The bringing of life into our hearts does not fix everything about us instantly. Regeneration gives the heart a new nature and the ability and desire to please God. However, this new ability is far from being the only impulse within us. Returning to our airplane analogy, once the nose of the airplane tilts downward, the inevitable end is a reunion with the ground. However, there is still a vast amount of atmosphere between the downward-traveling plane and the tarmac it will land upon. So it is with all of us who have experienced the new birth in our hearts. We have a long, long way to go.

The Bible teaches that we continue to struggle badly with sin because after regeneration two natures exist within us. The old, sinful nature has been dethroned, but it has not been cast out of the city gates of our hearts. It wages war against the new nature with a vengeance. The Christian heart is no idyllic vineyard scene, but is covered with the flotsam and grime of life in a war zone. We live perpetually vigilant, knowing that our Christian lives are the *continual* "taking off" of the sinful nature and "putting on" of the new nature that is in Christ (Eph. 4:22ff.).

But how exactly do these two competing natures exist within the biblical model of the heart? Answering this question will help make sense of heart change as a whole.

We must begin by recognizing that our former sinful nature

is us, but it is not our *identity*. Put differently, the old, sinful nature remains part of our hearts, but it is no longer the ruler of our hearts. It is an illegitimate insurgent, banished from the halls of power to haunt dark alleys and byways.

Think about your own experience of struggling with sinful thoughts, desires, and choices. These emerge out of *your* heart. They are not imposed from some outside source. Satan has not implanted in you a sudden desire to quarrel with your sibling, spouse, or friend. Rather, the desire to pick a fight is clearly connected with your desires. As James says, "Each person is tempted when he is drawn away and enticed by *his own* evil desire" (James 1:14). We need not look any further than our own hearts to see the source of our continued struggles with sin.

The apostle Paul captures our experience of this struggle so well in his extended agonizing over life with two natures in Romans 7. His "inner self" (i.e., his heart) delights in God's law (7:22), showing that he has a new heart which agrees with God rather than rebels against him. Yet, even though his heart is alive, he finds himself doing the very thing he hates. Put in heart language, he finds himself reasoning, desiring, and choosing contrary to the orientation of his heart. Paul wants to reason, desire, and choose righteously. And yet he bemoans the fact that "I do not do the good that I want to do, but I practice the evil that I do not want to do" (7:19).

Here we see Paul raise the critical matter of identity. Paul can very truly say, "But if I do the very thing I do not want, I am no longer the one doing it, but sin that dwells in me" (7:20 NASB). How exactly can Paul say that he is not the one sinning if the sin comes from his own heart? He can say this because "if anyone is in Christ, he is a new creation; the old has passed away, and . . . the new has come" (2 Cor. 5:17). Those who have experienced the new birth are indeed new creatures. We have a new Father. We are alive and not dead. We are in Christ rather than outside of him. We are adopted as sons and daughters. We are known by our covenant head's work on our behalf. This is our new identity; this is our new nature. There is no war for the throne of our hearts, there is no threat that the old nature may seize control and expel the new nature (see John 10:27–30). Every Christian is thoroughly a new creation. There is no question as to which nature will triumph.

However, even though the palace within our hearts remains secure, its streets remain dangerous places. Although righteousness reigns, there is an often vibrant underworld. These unrighteous crevices of our hearts are certainly still with us, as they exist within our hearts and we are our hearts. Paul is also very clear that though he is no longer his old nature, it is still he who operates unrighteously—"I practice the evil that I do not want to do" (Rom. 7:19). He does not distance himself from the old nature as though it was not him. It is indeed him, although it is no longer his identity and is fading away. We will return to explore this important theme in greater detail in chapter 5.

The Second Change: Sanctification

The conflict between the two natures leads us to the second kind of change that takes place within the heart. The first change, regeneration, changes the orientation of the heart as spiritual life bursts into existence. That change, however, is not the sum total of God's work within us.[35] The spark of life that is regeneration is only a beginning. Like any newborn, we are expected to grow up—into spiritual maturity. The author of Hebrews chides the church for its failure to grow beyond infancy:

> *We have a great deal to say about this, and it is difficult to explain, since you have become too lazy to understand. Although by this time you ought to be teachers, you need someone to teach you the basic principles of God's revelation again. You need milk, not solid food. Now everyone who lives on milk is inexperienced with the message about righteousness, because he is an infant. But solid food is for the mature—for those whose senses have been trained to distinguish between good and evil.*
>
> *(Heb. 5:11–14)*

The continued transformation of our hearts after they have sprung into spiritual life is referred to as "sanctification."[36]

While regeneration draws our attention to the new nature which has vivified our hearts, sanctification speaks to how we grow into spiritual maturity. Puritan Thomas Watson writes, "Sanctification is an intrinsic thing; it lies chiefly in the heart .... The dew wets the leaf, the sap is hid in the root; so the religion of some consists only in externals, but sanctification is deeply rooted in the soul."[37] As regeneration is the *rebirth* of the heart, sanctification is the continued *growth and maturation* of the heart.

Regeneration and sanctification are not the same thing, just as a child being born in the hospital is not the same thing as his or her growth over the next eighteen years of life. Being born is not the same thing as waving goodbye on the first day of school, skinning a knee on the playground, getting a driver's license, or going on a date. And yet, in order for any of those later events to happen, birth must first occur. Regeneration always precedes sanctification, and sanctification is the natural result of regeneration.

Sanctification and Heart Functions

Since sanctification is the renovation of the heart, we can expect our reasoning, desiring, and choosing to be significantly transformed over time as God's grace winds its way through our hearts. Thomas Watson helpfully explores the relationship between sanctification and changes in our heart functions:

> *After the fall, there was ignorance in the mind; but in sanctification, we are "light in the Lord" (Ephesians 5:8). After the fall, the will was depraved; there was not only impotence to good, but obstinacy. In sanctification, there is a blessed pliableness in the will; it symbolizes and comports with the will of God. After the fall, the affections were misplaced on wrong objects; in sanctification, they are turned into a sweet order and harmony, the grief placed on sin, the love on God, the joy on heaven. Thus sanctification spreads itself as far as original corruption; it goes over the whole soul.*[38]

Although Watson uses different terminology than we have used throughout our study (mind, affections, will), he rightly describes how spiritual growth impacts our reasoning, desiring, and choosing. Sanctification changes the functions of our hearts by changing the hearts from which the functions spring. As we grow in spiritual maturity, the outward expressions of our hearts slowly change as spiritual life progressively drives spiritual death from its safe houses within our hearts.

How Is Sanctification Change Brought About?[39]

Sanctifying change must not be thought of as a mystical process or a magical moment. I meet with many people who for years have yearned for their lives to change, yet have been stuck, making little to no progress. Almost invariably, their idea about how to change involves some kind of a "let go and let God" mentality. Paul corrects such a notion by urging us to "work out your own salvation with fear and trembling. For it is God who is working in you both to will and to work according to his good purpose" (Phil. 2:12–13). To riff off the words of one of my colleagues, sanctification is a product of "grace-driven effort."[40]

Petrus van Mastricht helpfully highlights the two overall means by which God sanctifies our hearts. We must "give our diligent and constant attention to the means which God customarily uses in this sanctification—the reading and hearing of the Word of God [and] conversation with the godly—and by these things to wait until at last it seems good to God, who commanded the light to shine out of darkness, to shine in our hearts."[41]

There certainly are other factors that God uses to transform our hearts. The breathtaking sweep of a three-mile stretch of craggy California coast named Montaña de Oro has frequently been a means of renewing my heart's joy and delight in God. However, the grandeur of nature itself is lost on me as a means of sanctification without the Word of God and conversation with the godly first opening my heart to see the coastline as revealing the grandeur and majesty of its creator.

Commenting on the specific trouble of anxiety, David Powlison observes that

> *there are countless ways to simply lessen anxiety: vigorous exercise, getting all the facts, Prozac, cognitive behavioral therapy, finding the best doctor, yoga, a vacation in*

> *Bermuda, a glass of wine, getting some distance from the problem, finding support from fellow sufferers, throwing yourself into work. Some of these are fine in their place. But none of them will make you fearless in the face of trouble .... None of them gives you high joy in knowing that your entire life is a holy experiment as God's hands shape you into the image of his Son. None of them changes the way you suffer by embedding it in deeper meaning.*[42]

We do well to identify the difference between the *primary* means of sanctification and a *secondary* means of sanctification. The primary way God changes our hearts, both in regeneration and in sanctification, is through the Word and Christian fellowship, which then give us the ability to rightly interpret other things around us, from the sweep of the sky to a baby's smile, in right ways that spur us on to greater faith and holiness.[43]

Tying It All Together

My friend Gavin[44] provides a very helpful portrait of how heart change plays out in an actual human life. Gavin first came to saving faith forty-five years ago. God changed his heart's orientation through regeneration due to the faithful witness of a pastor when Gavin was in his midtwenties.

Although his heart has been brought to spiritual life, Gavin's following four and a half decades have been marked by spiritual growth and continued struggles with anxiety, depression, and obsessive compulsions.

Gavin approached me one day after class and asked if I would be willing to counsel him. His reason for asking has stuck in my mind: "I've seen fourteen different mental health professionals and you're the first person who has ever mentioned that transformation is connected to our hearts."

Over a series of months, Gavin saw significant growth in his life through the application of God's Word to his heart and life. Prior therapy had been helpful for him to some degree, giving Gavin coping mechanisms to deal with the most paralyzing of his symptoms. Medications have helped stabilize some of the psychological vertigo he feels over even numbers, his front door lock, and decision-making. However, none of those has addressed the far weightier issues that wind through his troubles. Gavin has been most helped by engaging categories that are the chief domain of the Word of God:

- The difference between *feeling* guilty and actual guilt from breaking God's moral law;
- God's love for him in the midst of shame over being broken in ways most people don't understand;
- The rightness of feeling sad and discouraged over the deaths of several older relatives and the unjust breakup of his marriage of over forty years;
- Fighting intrusive thoughts with true statements anchored in God's sovereign ordering of his universe;
- Interrupting compulsions with faith-filled actions such as singing a hymn or writing out a prayer to God asking for help in the middle of his distress.

Gavin's sanctification has not been immediate. We've been working on slowly breaking free of compulsions, and we will probably continue to work for a significant amount of time. Our hearts often change slowly. And there certainly may be physiological factors that make Gavin's troubles far more difficult. But he is demonstrating change in his reasoning, his desires, and his choices. Heart change is producing change that is demonstrable.

Gavin still experiences significant distress at points. Some weeks are better than others, especially as he comes in contact with various triggers. In truth, he will likely experience distress until he dies and joins those who have finally been made fully new by our Lord. But the iron grip obsessions and compulsions have on his heart is loosening as the Lord is growing his heart.

5 A Significant Complication

Our previous two chapters have explored two different kinds of change people can experience. The first kind of change involves a change of lifestyle, but requires no change of heart. While such change can be lasting and real, it is independent of God's transforming work. The second kind of change, which we have called heart change, is the transformation of the heart itself, as the heart is brought to live through God's grace. That new life spreads throughout the heart as we are sanctified.

The easiest thing to do right now is simply skip to the final section of the book, which will focus on how to distinguish between these two kinds of change. We would have an easily memorable paradigm to apply: unbelievers experience lifestyle change, but Christians experience the deeper change within the heart's orientation, which is then expressed through a corresponding change in lifestyle. The problem is, while that paradigm would check all the boxes for being clean and trim, it wouldn't be honest.

Two Natures, One Complication

Our ability to clearly understand change is complicated by the fact that we have dueling natures after regeneration. Every Christian's heart has changed in its orientation, yet, as we noted in the previous chapter, every Christian's heart remains involved in its former rebellion. These two separate impulses within our hearts mean that change can originate from two very different drives. As Christians we *can* experience further heart change as God sanctifies us. However, we may also experience mere changes in lifestyle, derived from the sin nature that still resides within us as a very real expression of our hearts.

The cars most of us have sitting in our driveways provide a helpful example at this point. Fundamentally, we own cars in order for them to move us from one point to another. In order to do this, the engine converts gasoline into usable energy, which in turn powers the drivetrain and moves the car. However, not all movement in a car is a product of internal combustion. You may put your car in neutral and let it roll down a hill. If you break down, your car may be moved as a tow truck exerts an external force on your car. The fact that the car is moving is not proof that the engine is running.

So it is with our hearts. The fact that someone is a Christian and is changing is not a guarantee that such change is actually a change of heart. Regeneration and sanctification make further heart change *possible*, but the fact that God has graciously renovated our hearts does not guarantee that every change we experience going forward as a Christian is heart change.

Making Sense of Ourselves

The Bible introduces us to thousands of characters across its pages. While we may learn from all of them, the apostle Peter stands out as providing a template for considering the complicated way different changes interact within our hearts and lives. Peter's famous highs and lows reveal a man who is quite like us, capable of both great faith and great cowardice—often within just a few minutes of each other. We are inconsistent creatures, and the process of change within our hearts bears the stamp of our overall inconsistency.

Peter's experience of change from a fledgling follower of Jesus to a wise and valiant martyr-apostle gives us four windows to peer through to help us understand the messiness of the change that occurs within our own hearts. Overlap certainly exists between these different points, but each provides certain details that help us map ourselves.

1. The Overall Orientation of Our Hearts Has Changed, but We Continue to Struggle with a Virulent, Vibrant Sinful Nature in Many Specific Areas of Our Lives

The orientation of every Christian's heart has been changed through God's work of regeneration. That is, after all, what makes a Christian a Christian. We used to be at enmity with God, but now we are reconciled to him. We used to see the cross as foolish, but now we see it as the fountain of all our hope. While we used to scoff at God's commandments, we now see that true blessedness and flourishing comes through living as we were designed to live. Every Christian may repeat the refrain of the apostle Paul, "I have been crucified with Christ, and I no longer live, but Christ lives in me" (Gal. 2:20).

The change in heart orientation does not change everything about us. Until sanctification is complete, there is a virulent, seductive force within our soul that continues to call us to listen to it. And often we do—sometimes because we want to, sometimes by force of habit.

Peter's grandest moment in the Gospels is his declaration to Jesus, "You are the Messiah, the Son of the living God" (Matt. 16:16). Out of all of Jesus' followers, Peter puts together the pieces for the first time and declares Jesus to be the long-awaited fulfillment of all God's promises from Genesis to Malachi. Yet, Peter's very next words demonstrate the terribly unclear picture he has of what Jesus' messiahship means for him. He opposes Jesus' teaching about the Messiah's mission to die and rise again and gets himself called "Satan" in the process.

It's tempting to view Peter's troubles as simply being a product of imperfect knowledge. After all, he didn't fully grasp what it meant for Jesus to be the Messiah. However, Jesus' rebuke highlights that Peter's primary defect wasn't a lack of knowledge but a misguided heart: "You are a hindrance to me because you're not thinking about God's concerns but human concerns" (Matt. 16:23). David Turner draws out the collision between what God is calling Peter to believe and what Peter longs to be true:

> *Jesus' death is incompatible with Peter's notion of God's plan for the Messiah. Peter's Messiah is evidently the*

> *glorious Messiah who judges the world and reigns over it, not the one who suffers .... It is striking that in so short a time Peter has gone from being the rock-solid foundation on which Jesus will build the church to being a dangerous trap or stone over which Jesus may trip. This is due to Peter's mental fixation on human priorities, not divine revelation. Peter confesses Jesus as Messiah because of divine revelation, but he opposes Jesus's passion prediction because he thinks in line with human interests, not God's.*[45]

All of Peter's thoughts came from his heart, and the fact that he was willing to rebuke Jesus and declare a prophecy about his death wrong when it contradicted his view of what a Messiah ought to be showed in bright relief a heart that was significantly misguided. Peter's heart was committed to a reigning and conquering Messiah. Instead of saying, "Jesus, if you're going to die, please explain—I don't yet understand," he declared Jesus' plan to be wrong because it cut across his own presuppositions and life plan.

We see in Peter a man so much like us. Every Christian cries out with Peter that Jesus is indeed the Savior of the world. And yet, when it comes to our own lives, we often have enormous gaps between our acknowledgment of Christ's lordship and our willingness to follow him. We all read, "The LORD is my shepherd; I have what I need" (Ps. 23:1), but then murmur about the many things he has not given us. We embrace the idea of forgiveness, but are very slow to forgive. We love the concept of unity, but then define unity as "agreeing with me" rather than allowing for divergence of conscience (Rom. 14).

Each of these troubles is a product of the enduring sinful nature. Our orientation has changed, but inside the specifics, we consistently quarrel with Jesus.

2. We Are Inconsistent with Our Own Selves

Rarely do we see God's grace open our eyes to some further point of sanctification and never struggle again. Growth in any area of our lives is punctuated by great victories and tragic losses. If we imagine our hearts as an urban battlefield, there are many blocks which frequently change hands. There are moments when our hearts exude great character and righteousness, only to crumble the next moment. This does not automatically mean that such change was sourced only from self. Rather, it's the recognition that our faith often ebbs and flows. We may advance in righteousness and we may retreat. While our salvation is quite secure, our sanctification may fluctuate.

One of Peter's most spectacular collapses in life was actually preceded by a moment of great faith. The choppy Sea of Galilee was home to an old legend that before a boat would founder, it would be visited by a ghost walking across the waves.[46] As the disciples battled stiff headwinds one day, they looked up and were startled to see a ghostlike figure walking across the waves in the middle of the storm. To a man they cried out in terror, imagining themselves to be the legend's newest victims. Then Jesus reveals himself and Peter takes Jesus up on his charge to "have courage" and begins to walk on the water. We know how the story ends: Peter sees the winds and the waves, remembers that human beings are much too heavy for the tensile strength of the water's surface, and plunges beneath the waves (Matt. 14:22–32).

Peter is often chided as an example of little faith in this passage, but we must first remember the amount of courage he displayed in even getting out of the boat. Peter's initial faith in Jesus here wasn't a sham or a mirage. Jesus knew how to spot fake faith, and fake faith wouldn't have provided a firm footing for Peter's very first step. Jesus highlights Peter's "little faith" by asking, "Why did you doubt?" But doubt implies prior belief. Peter had faith and then he lost it under the assault of fear-inducing waves. His faith retreated as the wind-raked spray splashed across his brow.

Sanctification is a messy process in all of us. We have moments of great faith, and moments of embarrassing weakness. My first position as a counselor was in a college setting. My weekly schedule was often filled with young men struggling to overcome pornography addictions. Invariably, each man would experience moments of triumph and moments of failure. Temptation would strike and they would successfully resist through deeper desires for holiness and purity. The next time temptation struck, those exact same deep desires might prove to be much less compelling in the face of the strong desire to gratify lusts. They were inconsistent with themselves, valuing the same things quite differently at different times. Their gains were not fake and their losses were not a mirage. They were human beings in flux, caught in a war between dueling natures.

3. Genuine Growth in Our Hearts May Not Extend as Far as We Think It Does

We return to the apostle Peter, finding him lodging at Simon the Tanner's house. All of a sudden, Peter sees a vision from the Lord. A sheet descends from heaven full of animals that were unclean according to the Mosaic law. A voice commands Peter to kill and eat, and Peter, as a faithful Jew, protests. Then God responds by declaring, "What God has made clean, do not call impure" (Acts 10:15). Peter is perplexed about the meaning of the vision until a man enters the house asking him to come to Cornelius' house. Cornelius is a Gentile, and Peter suddenly understands what God meant through the vision.

When Peter enters Cornelius' house he publicly announces his understanding of the vision: "You know it's forbidden for a Jewish man to associate with or visit a foreigner, but God has shown me that I must not call any person impure or unclean" (10:28). He continues with even stronger words: "Now I truly understand that God doesn't show favoritism, but in every nation the person who fears him and does what is right is acceptable to him" (10:34–35). After Cornelius and all his household believe the gospel, Peter insists that they are to be baptized, the same as for Jewish believers—"Can anyone withhold water and prevent these people from being baptized, who have received the Holy Spirit just as we have?" (10:47). Including Gentiles as full and equal members in the fledgling church was radical, and Peter's support of the Gentiles kicked off an enduring controversy that would consume much of his energy.

Peter knows, loves, and chooses what is right in this scenario. His support of the Gentiles isn't a sham, but the true belief of a man who has heard from God and obeyed. The genuineness of Peter's belief is further shown by his willingness to stake his reputation and influence on the line at the Jerusalem Council, convened to settle once and for all the issue of Gentiles being included in the church. Peter strongly counters the argument of many Jewish leaders who insist that Gentiles must be circumcised, describing how God had chosen him specifically to proclaim the gospel to the Gentiles. In Peter's estimation, "God, who knows the heart, bore witness to them by giving them the Holy Spirit, just as he also did to us. He made no distinction between us and them, cleansing their hearts by faith" (Acts 15:8–9). Peter's transformation of heart is clear, from "No, Lord, I will not eat anything unclean," to being the most forceful advocate of Gentile inclusion.

And then, as we continue making our way through the Scriptures, we come across a curious account in Paul's letter to the churches in Galatia. While serving at the church in Antioch, Peter retreated from his former boldness. The apostle Paul relates the tense encounter between the two apostles:

> *But when Cephas [i.e., Peter] came to Antioch, I opposed him to his face because he stood condemned. For he regularly ate with the Gentiles before certain men came from James. However, when they came, he withdrew and separated himself, because he feared those from the circumcision party. Then the rest of the Jews joined his hypocrisy, so that even Barnabas was led astray by their hypocrisy. But when I saw that they were deviating from the truth of the gospel, I told Cephas in front of everyone, "If you, who are a Jew, live like a Gentile and not like a Jew, how can you compel Gentiles to live like Jews?"*
>
> *(Gal. 2:11–14)*

There is genuine growth within Peter. Paul notes that Peter himself "live[s] like a Gentile." Peter has not retreated back to his days before the sheet descended from heaven. He has not returned to a fully Jewish way of life. But, under the withering pressure of powerful men, Peter withdrew from fully including the Gentiles in fellowship. Philip Ryken helpfully notes, "What Peter did was not a matter of principle; it was a case of cowardice."[47] Peter is not renouncing his former beliefs; rather, he's now living as a hypocrite. He has changed, but he hasn't changed as much as we (or he) might have imagined. His courage hasn't grown quite as much as his doctrine.

This pattern extends beyond the pages of Scripture to our own lives. David and Krista Dunham's *Table for Two* recounts her decade-long struggle with anorexia. Their narrative poignantly captures Krista's fits and starts as she wrestles with complex motives within her heart. For a long season of life she grows, but doesn't grow *that* much. Her words ring true for all of us, whatever sinful struggles we face: "Although I was on the path to recovery back then, it turned out to be longer than I realized in the moment and harder than I was able to deal with on my own. Along the way, there was a recurring pattern: I constantly thought I was doing better than I really was."[48] We are all on the path of growth, but often our footfalls are several steps behind where we think we are. Those seasons of collapse cause us to return and strengthen foundations that couldn't quite hold the weight we thought they could.

4. We Will Never Have Entirely Transformed Hearts During Our Earthly Life

Although this is a book about heart transformation, we do well to remind ourselves of the nature of our entire life on earth. We are terribly inconsistent, even to our dying days. Although we grow in godliness, we will never reach a place where every block of our heart has been sanctified and entirely rid of insurgents who wage war against us. At the end of his life, the apostle Paul could simultaneously say with confidence, "I have fought the good fight, I have finished the race, I have kept the faith," and "if we are faithless, he remains faithful, for he cannot deny himself" (2 Tim. 4:7–8; 2:13).

One of the great hopes for the future lies in the knowledge that our hearts will finally be trustworthy once our bodies have been laid in the grave and our souls are with the Lord. The early church father Ignatius of Antioch wrote a letter to the church in Rome while being transported there to be martyred. In a play on words, Ignatius begged the Roman church not to intervene, but rather to let him die so that he might live: "Pardon me, brethren: do not hinder me from living, do not wish to keep me in a state of death; and while I desire to belong to God, do not give me over to the world. Allow me to obtain pure light: when I have gone there, I shall indeed be a man of God."[49] For Ignatius, continued life on earth was continuing in a state of death when compared with the life that he was to gain with Christ.

I often find myself wondering exactly how much of my own

godliness is sourced from a transformed heart, and how much of it is a smoke-and-mirrors product of the old nature. If Satan himself can appear as an angel of light, surely too our exhibitions of righteousness may appear to be not what we imagined them to be.

We may know that we are Christians. The apostle John summarizes his first epistle saying, "I have written these things to you who believe in the name of the Son of God so that you may *know* that you have eternal life" (1 John 5:13). Our own inconsistencies are not meant to drive us to doubt that we are Christ's.

However, we must also acknowledge that our security in our expressions of godliness needs to be much less than our confidence in our salvation. Peter would have seemed far holier had the Judaizers never arrived. But the Judaizers simply pointed out latent hypocrisy inside his heart. What similar subterranean caverns exist within my own heart? Within yours? Within the hearts of those we seek to help? It is difficult to know in a life where the most extreme trials are (thankfully!) not a constant reality.

What if Peter had come to the end of his life and never been tested by such intense Jewish pressure? What if his hypocrisy had never been exposed, and his heart transformation was much shallower than he thought?

What would have happened is that Peter would still have been martyred, he would have been received into glory, and he would have experienced full and final sanctification, where his heart would have been made entirely pure and he no longer would experience the oh-so-frustrating experience of being a fractured human being, struggling with sin, and struggling with struggling with sin. When all is said and done, our security before God does not lie in our self-knowledge, but in his love for us. That beautiful truth enables Paul to encourage believers to trust God with the rapidity of their own sanctification: "I pursue as my goal the prize promised by God's heavenly call in Christ Jesus. Therefore, let all of us who are mature think this way. And if you think differently about anything, God will reveal this also to you. In any case, we should live up to whatever truth we have attained" (Phil. 3:14–16).

We are called to walk forward in faithfulness, knowing that

God will reveal to us those places where heart transformation has not occurred to the degree we think it has. And, when those times happen, we now have a higher standard of truth which we have attained. We do well to remember that God is patient and kind with poor stragglers like us all.

Part III

Distinguishing between Kinds of Change

6 How Can You Tell?

Most of the people I interact with throughout the day are students harried by all the busyness that is grad school. Typical get-to-know-you questions such as "What are your hobbies?" or "What do you do in your spare time?" tend to get the same answer—"I don't have spare time." Or, in the case of some delightfully sparky student, "Read all the books that you've assigned me." Rock climbing, painting, woodworking, and the like tend to get crowded out by more pressing matters such as actually passing classes.

The uniformity of these responses motivated me to come up with a better introductory question: "What do you know more about than you ought to?" You learn all kinds of things about people this way, as everybody is a nerd about something. I discovered one well-known theologian has a weakness for the Discovery Channel's Shark Week. One of my students has a past history of potato farming. It's always amazing to hear the detailed and specific knowledge people have accumulated through their life experiences.

My answer to this question is "rabbit breeding." I've raised rabbits for several years, including working to rehabilitate a heritage breed which has become endangered. While rabbits live up to their reputation for breeding prolifically, baby rabbits (called "kits") also have a high fatality rate. It's not unusual for 25 percent of any litter to perish before six weeks of age. I'm often surprised by which kits make it and which ones don't. Sometimes the rabbits that appear healthiest succumb to unseen neurological or gastrointestinal issues, or get separated from the needed warm places in the nest. And sometimes, the smallest rabbit that looks a step or two away from death's door winds up excelling all its siblings. The only thing that can be said about any individual kit is that time will tell.

Time Will Tell

"Time will tell" also serves as the motto for discerning what kind of change is taking place within an individual's life. As finite beings, we are locked into time and space and know what will happen in the future only when time passes and what was once future is now present. We all know those who appeared to possess a great zeal for the Lord in high school, college, or beyond, yet eventually fell away from the faith into apostasy. The lack of heart change within them became apparent only with the passing of time.

Our knowledge is limited by our inability to know the motivations that drive an individual's transformation. Not all enduring change is a change of heart; as we've seen before, people can change in their thoughts, desires, and actions without actually experiencing a change of heart. How can we know if an angry man's new peaceful demeanor is driven by love to God and neighbor, or by self-interest so his wife will not leave him (which is a fine motivation, but not an ultimate motivation)?

When an angry man starts acting peaceably and kindly toward his wife, has he changed from the heart? Or has he simply changed his behavior out of self-interest and a fear of divorce (Phil. 2:3–4)? Are a woman's laudable steps away from addiction civic righteousness or produced by the Holy Spirit's conviction and renovation of her soul? As finite beings, we lack the equipment necessary to peer into the deepest part of a person and find answers to these kinds of questions. As the Scriptures state, "Humans see what is visible, but the Lord sees the heart" (1 Sam. 16:7).

A Conundrum

The thesis of this book, that there are two different kinds of change that human beings can undergo, has brought us to a conundrum. We have seen how the first kind of change, change in a heart's operations or expressions, is an observable change in someone's reasoning, desires, and choices. They have changed their mind, changed their loves, and changed their choices. This kind of change is readily apparent to us as we are able to hear, see, and experience it.

However, the deeper level of change, what we've called "heart change," is also expressed through the heart's operations. This kind of change is produced only through God's gracious work on the heart, which is ultimately inaccessible to our eyes. What we *can* see of heart change is the transformation of someone's reasoning, desires, and choices.

But that leaves us stuck, as the observable proofs of heart change are the same as the evidence for operation change that requires no change of heart. What are we to do? Are there any kinds of tests or evidence that might give us a hint as to what kind of change has occurred? Answering this question is critical for every human being, as there are many who think they have changed from the heart, yet are heading toward a tragic collision with Jesus declaring "I never knew you. Depart from me" (Matt. 7:23). It's also a critical question for counselors to answer, as our ultimate aim is to help people experience genuine heart transformation for their good and God's glory.

Uncovering False Assurances of Heart Change

Before we work through two positive identifying marks of heart change, it's important to sweep away several pieces of evidence that we are prone to mistakenly identify as proof. We are not the first generation of Christians to travel these paths and we are wise to listen to the voices of those who have gone before us. Perhaps the most enduringly helpful voice in this conversation is that of Jonathan Edwards (1703–1758), a colonial pastor, missionary, and college president. Edwards was a major figure in the First Great Awakening, a time of unparalleled evangelistic success in the American colonies. Almost every person in Edwards' town of Northampton made a profession of faith in Jesus Christ. Yet, less than twenty years later, Edwards mourned that many, if not most, of the converts during this revival ultimately reverted to their distinctly non-Christian lifestyles and beliefs.[50] Edwards put pen to paper in a treatise called *Religious Affections* in an attempt to help his congregation and other Christians across the globe evaluate whether or not the changes they saw in their thinking, desires, and choices were evidence of heart transformation or merely change brought about by self-effort.

Edwards begins by identifying several evidences that are not proof of heart transformation. His list is unnerving as it cuts across many of our imagined safe harbors. And yet, his work endures because of how truly and biblically he has analyzed our human experience.

Five Unreliable Evidences of Heart Change

Myth #1: Intensity of Feeling Is Proof of Faith

The first unreliable evidence that Edwards identifies is that of feelings. Edwards rightly insisted that loving God consists of more than just intellectual appreciation. In contrast with some of his contemporaries, Edwards emphasized how genuine faith stirs the heart to joyful feelings as people are moved by God's goodness and kindness. Historical accounts recall that people would cry, shout, and moan during Edwards' preaching—very unusual responses for that day. Edwards' own wife, Sarah, fell into some kind of rapturous trance for two weeks, consumed with intense feelings of devotion and love for God.

While Edwards saw these intense feelings as good and right, he also insisted that feelings and emotions do not *constitute faith*. He reminded those in his charge that:

- "It is no sign, one way or the other, that religious affections are very great, or raised very high" (II.1).[51]
- "It is no sign that affections have the nature of true religion … that they have great effects on the body" (II.2).
- "Nothing can be certainly concluded concerning the nature of religious affections, that … the relation persons give of them, are very affecting" (II.12).

While joy, zeal, happiness, and other intense emotions may be products of genuine faith, they are not proof that a person's heart has actually changed.

Those of us who are involved in caring for people see white-hot emotion regularly. I do not have hard statistics for such things, but I probably see more men and women dissolve into tears than most folk, given my profession. People are overcome by emotion due to pain and suffering, conviction over their sin, and seeing new glories in God that previously escaped their view.

Crises are by nature times of greatly heightened emotions. People often vacillate between the deepest bogs and the highest peaks. In moments of crisis, conviction of sin may be deeper, pain from suffering may be darker, and the fires that drive motivation to change may glow with a fierce intensity. As encouraging as fresh zeal may be, we are wise to remember that the strength of someone's feelings is no proof that whatever changes follow come from a transformed heart.

When I was in seminary one day, a neighbor pulled me aside and shared how God had been powerfully impressing on his heart the need to put to death his secret pornography habit. He spoke with great feeling of how the past week had been one of physically trembling and weeping as his soul was consumed with horror over how greatly he had offended God and his wife. A week after graduation that same neighbor was exposed as having had a yearlong affair with a coworker.

One counselee sat in my office and spoke with passion and joy of how his new understanding of the doctrine of election had completely changed the game in his battle against depression. He too later made shipwreck of his life, identifying that doctrine he once rejoiced in as actually fueling his drug use and adulteries.

These two stories are only two of many, and if you've ministered to people for any length of time I know you and I could fill a book with plenty more. Rapturous experiences of joy, white-hot zeal, grief over sin—none is a proof of heart transformation. Scripture is littered with the shattered remains of strong passion that fell by the wayside. King Jeroboam, King Joash, King Jehu. Esau, Judas, Demas. All possessed a glowing fire of feeling that cooled into a heart of stone.

Myth #2: Enjoying Conversations about God, His Works, and His Word Is Proof of Faith

The first unreliable evidence identified by Edwards focused on affections. This second myth turns an eye toward knowledge. Edwards noticed that many individuals who once used their time to contemplate theology and their mouths to speak of things of God did not endure in faith. His words are haunting:

- "Nothing can be certainly known of the nature of religious affections . . . that they much dispose persons with their mouths to praise and glorify God" (II.10).
- "It is no sign that affections are truly gracious . . . that they cause those who have them to be fluent, fervent, and abundant, in talking of the things of religion" (II.3).

"Talk is cheap" goes one cultural phrase, and this is no less true in holy things than in the commonplace. Who can ignore the list of men once considered eloquent heroes of the faith who have been fired, defrocked, or disgraced for the most terrible of sins, proclaiming the excellencies of God with one part of their lives, and living as enemies of the cross with the other?

I use these men as examples because of their very public speech about God and his glory. Of course, a love of theology that masks a deep lack of virtue isn't a trouble just for Christian celebrities; it's a trouble for people in every place. We all know men and women whose words turned out to be a false flag. Coworkers, friends, family members, children, spouses, mentors, pastors—all may speak wonderful truths about God, yet ultimately be entirely unmoved within their hearts.

Theological knowledge and an ability to talk about who God is, what he has done, and what he desires us to do is beneficial for us as people. We are called to move beyond elementary things into the deeper doctrines of the Christian faith. Doing so is for our good as we see more of God's glory, experience more of his comfort, and overcome sin which clings to us. However, we cannot mistake that knowledge and speech for proof of a transformed heart. To do so is to confuse the kindling with the flame. Biblical and theological knowledge fuels the fire of heart transformation as the Spirit uses the Word to renovate the deepest parts of who we are as people. But the knowledge itself is mere kindling, with no inherent warmth in itself when housed in a cold heart.

Myth #3: Love for the Scriptures, the Church, and Fellow Christians Is Proof of Faith

Our third mythological "proof" of heart transformation looks at the habits and disciplines that are part of living as a Christian. Edwards noticed that a person's commitment to reading the Scriptures, participating in church worship meetings, and acts of love and service to others were not indications that any movement had occurred within that person's heart. As he put it:

- "It is no sign that religious affections are truly holy and spiritual . . . that they come with texts of Scripture, remarkably brought to the mind" (II.5).
- "It is no certain sign that the religious affections . . . have in them the nature of true religion . . . that they dispose persons to spend much time in religion, and to be zealously engaged in the external duties of worship" (II.9).
- "It is no evidence that religious affections are saving . . . that there is an appearance of love in them" (2.6).

As with our two previous myths, these desires and acts are good and necessary products of a transformed heart. I am concerned about a heart that is never affected by Scripture, just as with a person who avoids gathering together with the church to worship God, fellowship, and serve. However, these *products* of heart transformation should not be taken as *proof* that heart transformation has occurred. All may be produced by self-effort without any actual change of heart.

Sadly, the two most difficult counselees I have ever had were a pastor and a missionary. The pastor preached almost weekly for half a decade. The missionary had uprooted his life in service of the poor in another country. Yet for all the hours and sacrifices they had made, there was no heart transformation. They sacrificed for Jesus and screamed at their wives, preached and punched holes in the walls of their homes.

No grace from God is required to be moved by David and Jonathan's friendship, by Ruth's service, by Esther's courage.

God need not work in someone's heart for that person to read through the Bible in a year, sit in church, sing hymns, teach Sunday school, bring people meals, or go on missions trips. While these "external duties of worship" naturally flow from a transformed heart, a transformed heart is not the only motivator of such actions.

Myth #4: Confidence in God's Work Is Proof of Faith

The fourth category of unreliable proofs looks at a person's own thoughts about their transformation. Edwards noticed that many people who were absolutely confident that God had worked to transform their hearts later slid back into their former patterns of life. In Edwards' words:

- "It is no sign that affections are right, or that they are wrong, that they make persons that have them exceeding confident that what they experience is divine" (II.11).

One of the most quoted verses from the Old Testament reminds us how unreliable we are as interpreters of our own experience. Jeremiah 17:9 tells the sad truth that "the heart is more deceitful than anything else, and incurable—who can understand it?" Our perception of what occurs within our own hearts is fractured by the sin that exists within it. We are like a shattered windshield, with spidery cracks that run to and fro obscuring the landscape in front of us.

The Bible holds a very dim view of our ability to rightly discern what is happening within our own hearts. Consider the following testimonies:

- "There is a way that seems right to a person, but its end is the way to death" (Prov. 14:12).

- "While he was in Jerusalem during the Passover Festival, many believed in his name when they saw the signs he was doing. Jesus, however, would not entrust himself to them, since he knew them all and because he did not need anyone to testify about man; for he himself knew what was in man" (John 2:23–25).

- "Not everyone who says to me, 'Lord, Lord,' will enter

> the kingdom of heaven, but only the one who does the will of my Father in heaven. On that day many will say to me, 'Lord, Lord, didn't we prophesy in your name, drive out demons in your name, and do many miracles in your name?' Then I will announce to them, 'I never knew you. Depart from me, you lawbreakers!'" (Matt. 7:21–23).

Is it any wonder the Bible commands us to "trust in the LORD with all your heart, and do not rely on your own understanding" (Prov. 3:5)?

Edwards rightly recognized that men and women are often very confident that the Lord must be working in their hearts because there are new thoughts, desires, and choices that did not seem to come from their own efforts. They feel conviction without getting caught, or want to change without first hitting the misery of rock bottom.

Anyone who ministers to others and is in relationship with people who struggle with habitual and repeated sin, be it substance abuse, matters of sexual purity, financial stewardship, or a host of other things, instantly recognizes in Edwards' older English the echo of words they hear all the time: "I've really changed this time. Something's different. God's done something in me."

The Holy Spirit certainly does convict people, and he really does change people. Behind every heart change is the truth that something *is* different this time. However, Edwards wants to help those looking on from the outside to remember that a person's confidence does not equal a genuine work of God in renovating the heart. It might be so, but as with the previous signs, confidence in its own right does not mean that the heart has changed.

Myth #5: Statements of Desiring Change Are Proof of Faith

The final myth is one I'd like to add to Edwards' time-honored observations. People who are stuck and in pain will often say some version of "I'll do anything" to fix their struggle with anger, a treasured relationship gone sour, or an enslaving sinful habit. They express, often strongly, a desire to change.

While I have no doubt that the person genuinely desires to

move past his or her troubles, "I'll do anything" often excludes the very thing that needs changing—the person uttering the phrase.

More than one counselee has started meeting with me by passionately insisting that they are absolutely broken and want nothing more than to submit totally to God's Word. Indeed, many love the *idea* of being convicted by the Scriptures more than they like actual conviction, which requires letting go of their autonomy, control, and whatever aspects of life fuel their specific trouble.

C. S. Lewis' poignant tale in *The Great Divorce* of the Ghost with the red lizard on his shoulder captures this dynamic extremely well. The red lizard (understood to be a particularly enslaving vice) torments the Ghost and drives him mad. Yet, at the moment he would be free, the Ghost finds himself unsure. The book's protagonist captures the exchange between his angel-guide and the lizard keeper:

> *"Would you like me to make [the lizard] quiet?" said the flaming Spirit—an Angel as I now understood.*
>
> *"Of course I would," said the Ghost.*
>
> *"Then I will kill him," said the Angel, taking a step forward.*
>
> *"Oh—ah—look out! You're burning me. Keep away," said the Ghost, retreating.*
>
> *"Don't you want him killed?"*
>
> *"You didn't say anything about killing him at first. I hardly meant to bother you with anything so drastic as that."*
>
> *"It's the only way," said the Angel .... "May I kill it?"*
>
> ...
>
> *"Well, there's time to discuss that later."*
>
> *"There is no time. May I kill it?"*
>
> *"Please, I never meant to be such a nuisance. Please—really—don't bother. Look! It's gone to sleep of its own accord. I'm sure it'll be all right now. Thanks ever so much."*
>
> *"May I kill it?"*[52]

There is no way around it: heart change is most often difficult, painful, and costly. An angry man who protects himself and orders his life through bullying, fear, and intimidation must become someone different. And that requires the relinquishing of the very things that he has invested in and used to keep himself happy and safe. People in misery most often do desire change; however, that desire is often paired with great fear over parting with troubles that have fused with their identity.

Jesus recognized this ambivalence that is natural to human beings. As popular support for his ministry began to swell, Jesus turned to the "great crowds" who were following him with a stark message:

> *Whoever does not bear his own cross and come after me cannot be my disciple.*
>
> *For which of you, wanting to build a tower, doesn't first sit down and calculate the cost to see if he has enough to complete it? … In the same way, therefore, every one of you who does not renounce all his possessions cannot be my disciple.*
>
> (*Luke 14:27–28, 33*)

Not everyone is ready to change from the heart. The cost will be high, and statements declaring a strong desire to change must be followed by an enduring willingness to bear the cross, pay the price, and see it through.

Perplexed? Me Too

The first time I read *Religious Affections*, I found myself wondering what exactly then could be considered proofs of actual change. Edwards pulled the rug out from under all the evidences I typically trusted in as marks of authentic heart transformation in myself and others. Perhaps your experience is similar. But before we throw up our hands and surrender to agnosticism about whether or not we can know anything about the kind of change that's occurring within someone, we do well to look more deeply. Edwards, after all, wrote *Religious Affections* to help people identify true marks of heart transformation and give them assurance of the work God was doing within their souls.

Proofs of Heart Change

Despite its warnings of false assurance, Scripture is also quite certain that marks of genuine heart transformation exist and may be identified. Out of all sixty-six books in the Bible, the small book of 1 John treats the concept of certainty most clearly. Consider the following words:

- "This is how *we know* that *we know* him: if we keep his commands" (1 John 2:3).
- "*We know* that we have passed from death to life because we love our brothers and sisters" (1 John 3:14).
- "The way *we know* that he remains in us is from the Spirit he has given us" (1 John 3:24).
- "*We know* that we are of God, and the whole world is under the sway of the evil one" (1 John 5:19).
- "*We know* that the Son of God has come and has given us understanding so that we may know the true one. We are in the true one—that is, in his Son, Jesus Christ. He is the true God and eternal life" (1 John 5:20).

These five verses (and others) all share the same theme—*we know* that we are in Christ. To put it in the language of this book, *we know* that our hearts have been transformed. We may know that we are regenerate. And by that we may also know that we are being sanctified.

Two marks in particular emerge from the pages of Scripture that indicate observable change is sourced from the heart. These two marks are not an either/or proposition, but rather work together in tandem to provide evidence that heart transformation is occurring. We must remember that evidence is just that—there always exists the possibility that an overwhelming amount of contrary evidence exists that we cannot see. However, all things being equal, these two marks provide trustworthy evidence that observable change is happening from the heart.

Mark #1: Endurance

The first mark that helps us distinguish between heart change and mere change in the heart's expressions is *endurance*. Now, this mark by itself is no proof of heart change. We noted earlier that non-Christians may certainly experience lasting change. However, any transformation that does not endure is clearly not due to a renovation of the heart. Durability opens the possibility of legitimacy.

We as people generally have the ability to transform ourselves by our own effort for a short amount of time. We can hold back our temper from a senior manager at work. We can clean up our language around a pastor or disapproving family member. We can present perfectly manicured houses (and families) when someone from church comes over. An entirely unchurched young woman may become suddenly quite devout when a young man of interest makes clear such things are important to him. Still other changes are genuinely well intentioned, but fade just the same.

The Scriptures tie the proof of heart transformation very closely to endurance. Jesus assured his listeners that "the one who endures to the end will be saved" (Matt. 24:13). The apostle James expands on Jesus' teaching: "Consider it a great joy, my brothers and sisters, whenever you experience various trials, because you know that the testing of your faith produces endurance. And let endurance have its full effect, so that you may be mature and complete, lacking nothing" (James 1:2–4). Paul writes to the church in Galatia, "Let us not get tired of doing good, for we will reap at the proper time if we don't give up" (Gal. 6:9).

Endurance is one essential piece of heart transformation because time allows for our hearts to be tested in many ways. There are six particular ways in which time challenges perceived heart change:

First, time allows for continued interest to be demonstrated. Novelty easily keeps us engaged for a short amount of time. Most of our garages are littered with exercise equipment, fancy coffee roasting equipment, or materials for craft projects. All began with sincerity and the best of intentions, but as excitement gave way to the daily grind, they fell below the horizon line and were forgotten. A transformed heart's values have been transformed, creating a durability of change. As Jesus says, "Where your treasure is, there your heart will be also" (Matt. 6:21).

Second, time allows for disappointment in ourselves to

occur. As noted in the previous chapter, we are inconsistent people at best, and it's easy to grow disappointed in our continued struggles and failures. As people with hearts that enfold two different natures, we will inevitably fall short of our own expectations. Proverbs contrasts well the responses to failure of a transformed heart and an untransformed heart: "Though a righteous person falls seven times, he will get up, but the wicked will stumble into ruin" (Prov. 24:16).

One bad week has proven to be the graveyard of many diets and Bible reading plans. Every process of change involves moving forward, falling back, discouragement, resolve, prayer, and faith. Genuine heart change is marked by endurance because a changed heart is compelled to strive for righteousness.

Third, time gives opportunity for righteous stubbornness in the face of headwinds created by others. We are all embedded in relationships, and the fact that *I* may desire to change does not automatically mean that *others* share that goal. Change can often be a lonely road to walk. I've counseled many men and women in unhappy marriages whose desire to create a joyful marriage through obedience to the Lord has been rebuffed by an uninterested spouse. These moments reveal whether the desire for change is sourced from heart transformation or is dependent upon the behavior of others.

Fourth, time allows for endurance to persevere in the midst of suffering. Paul aptly states, "For we know that the whole creation has been groaning together with labor pains until now" (Rom. 8:22). Our world is red in tooth and claw, and we inhabit this world in bodies that are breaking down as we slowly wind our way toward death and a return to the dust.

Every son of Adam and daughter of Eve will suffer. Given enough time, that suffering permeates every category of life as there is no corner of our lives that is left unscathed by personal sin, the sins of others, or the troubles of living in a broken world. Chronic pain, economic disaster, the sudden death of a child—all are temptations to abandon the pursuit of righteousness. Those whose hearts have been changed endure through their tears, for neither hell nor high water can shake what the Spirit has done within a person's heart.

Fifth, time allows for other enticing things to arise. Change is harder than the status quo, and there are many other glittering things that call to our hearts. Easy sex offers pleasure, and promises to be a cure for loneliness, especially when compared with patiently bearing up under the weight of undesired singleness. The siren call of blameshifting offers a shortcut to getting rid of guilt while preserving one's dignity when compared with an admission of failure and humble repentance. As time moves onward, we see a growing collection of rejected temptations pile up in the rearview mirror of our hearts.

Sixth, time allows for us to come to terms with the reality of who God is. The God who actually exists and the God we *want* to exist often do not see eye to eye. Time allows for moments of crisis to arise when these two different visions collide. When the chips are down, are we willing to bow before the Father alongside Jesus and say, "Not as I will, but as you will" (Matt. 26:39)?

As I get to know new counselees I usually ask, "What have you done to try to solve your problems so far?" Almost all of them answer, "Pray that God would take them away." That God has not done so often fuels resentment toward him or distrust of his goodness. But the Lord does not usually work by suddenly taking away our troubles. His normal pattern of care consists of growing us to be able to live righteously in the midst of difficulty. How a person responds in these moments is a powerful test of what kind of change is occurring within his or her heart.

These six challenges and enticements provide a landscape for change to be evaluated. Heart change will endure because it comes from the grace-infused heart. It is a tree that fears no drought because its roots are sunk deep into the subterranean living water that is Jesus Christ and his active work in the heart through his Spirit. In the words of John Newton,

Through many dangers, toils, and snares
I have already come:
'Tis grace has brought me safe thus far,
And grace will lead me home.

('Amazing Grace')

Heart change endures.

Mark #2: Whole-Life Integrity

Endurance alone does not automatically prove that any observed change comes from the heart. Addicts can walk away from substances and never touch them again without setting foot inside a church. A philanderer can become and remain faithful apart from God's gracious intervention in his life. A woman consumed with anxiety may gain confidence to live well in her world without opening a Bible. Endurance *alone* does not indicate that the transformation that's taking place is an actual renovation or growth in the heart.

This leads to the second mark of heart transformation: whole-life integrity. Individual changes that take place within a person exist within the much larger context of the person's entire life. One needs only to watch the headlines for a few months to add more names to the list of wealthy men and women who are simultaneously philanderers and philanthropists. The goodness of eradicating malaria, creating enduring pieces of art, or seeking to redress injustice does not tip the scales in the person's favor, as goodness in one category of life does not erase the necessity of goodness in all categories of life. As Thomas Watson helpfully describes the extent of such change: "a good Christian, though he be sanctified but in part, yet in every part."[53]

The cornerstone of whole-life integrity is a belief in the gospel of Jesus Christ. To return to a previous point, "those who are in the flesh cannot please God" (Rom. 8:8). While only God can see the heart, we can hear and evaluate an individual's profession of faith. If someone does not profess faith in Christ Jesus, we can be certain that whatever change has happened or is happening does not spring from a transformed heart.

Because heart change is a change in our heart's orientation which then pushes itself into the heart's expressions, there are no corners of our lives which are left entirely untouched by the Lord. Regeneration means that there is a new force on the throne of the heart. The new nature is backed by Christ's authority, which is absolute (Matt. 28:18). There is no line drawn in a regenerate heart that says, "Jesus Christ may come this far, but no farther."

This certainly is not to say that Christians do not struggle with sin. The apostle James affirms divine truth and our own experience as he writes in the present tense, "We all stumble in many ways" (James 3:2). For those who do profess to follow Christ, genuine transformation of heart takes place within the larger context of a faithful life. Obedience and patterns of righteousness are entirely required for the observed change to be the product of a changed heart. Believers will certainly stumble and fall, and believers may certainly engage in lengthy battles (sometimes lifelong battles) with sin and temptation. However, the Bible's expectation is that Christ will have all of us. The Rich Young Ruler's righteous lifestyle was unmasked as mere pretense when Jesus asked him to give up his most treasured category—his treasure.

These two factors, endurance and whole-life integrity, weave together to provide confidence that the changes we observe come from the heart. Do they provide an infallible test? Certainly not. Even some elders who were appointed in the church of Ephesus because of their apparently godly character turned out to be savage wolves (Acts 20:29). But those who endure to the end, their godliness tested and refined by the fires of time, have every right to be confident that their hearts are being transformed.

7 A Parable Paints a Portrait

This small work on the nature of how we change as human beings has talked quite a bit in theological categories. These categories are clear and defined, but life as it is actually lived often muddies the process. As one of my professors was fond of saying, "Life is more complicated than reading."

One of Jesus' parables helps us think through how theology like this comes to bear on our actual lives. "The parable of the sower" (Matt. 13:3–9, 18–23) is known as such because of its first line—"Consider the sower who went out to sow." However, a name that better captures the point of Jesus' teaching is "the parable of the four soils," as the parable focuses on the seed's reaction to different kinds of soil rather than on the person who is casting the seed about. The soil is specifically mentioned as representing the "heart" (13:19). Thus, this parable is a window into four different ways the human heart responds to calls to change.

A Biblical Portrait of Kinds of Change

Perhaps because of its traditional name, the parable of the four soils is usually thought of in terms of how people respond to evangelistic gospel presentations. Some reject the gospel, some profess faith but later fall away for various reasons, and some endure and bear much fruit. This reading of the parable is certainly appropriate, but there's no reason to restrict this parable to only that application. The seed scattered is the "word" (Mark 4:14) or more specifically the "word about the kingdom"(Matt. 13:19). In other words, the parable is about how our hearts respond to the message of Jesus. The message of Jesus is far more than belief in and assent to the gospel. It's a message that permeates every category of our lives. The word of the kingdom does not suddenly cease to be the vehicle for change once we've accepted Christ. Indeed, the saving message is the sanctifying message. When we read the parable of the four soils through the lens of heart change, we see something surprising. The four different soils described by Jesus map perfectly onto the different kinds of change we have walked through in the preceding pages.

Seed #1: Snatched by the Birds

The first soil Jesus describes is the inhospitable path. Because the word of the kingdom—the only thing that can create heart change—is left open and exposed, passing birds, who are identified with the devil, may easily peck away at what would otherwise germinate. However, before we careen away into blaming a lack of change solely on demonic influence, we must remember that the soil is the heart of a person. The devil may snatch the truth away only because hard-heartedness has compacted the heart and left the seed exposed and vulnerable. D. A. Carson describes this relationship well: "Jesus' interpretation is clear: Some people hear the message about the kingdom, but like hardened paths, they do not let the truth penetrate; before they really understand it the devil has snatched it away."[54]

This category maps onto situations where growth simply never occurs. Many remain willfully ignorant regarding their need to change. One of my counselees had been recalled from the mission field by his sending church, censured by a new church, and then had the same issues addressed in counseling. Yet, he refused to acknowledge his need for change, and invested all his energy into jeremiads against those he thought had wronged him. Still others know they need to change, but lifelong patterns have hardened their hearts. Though there is light, there is no softness for that knowledge to penetrate deeply and germinate.

Regenerate and unregenerate hearts may both be hard

packed and inhospitable to change. For an unbeliever, such hardness is only natural. For the believer, we know that hardness remains in even the softest heart. The apostle Paul bewailed his enduring hardness: "For I do not understand what I am doing, because I do not practice what I want to do, but I do what I hate" (Rom. 7:15). Elsewhere, he would remind us that we have not already reached full spiritual maturity, but can know that "if you think differently about anything, God will reveal this also to you. In any case, we should live up to whatever truth we have attained" (Phil. 3:15–16). Those places where we have yet to grow as we ought remain hard packed. But God in his time is slowly cultivating the field that is our hearts, breaking up tough clods that plants may grow.

Seed #2: Scorched by the Sun

The second soil Jesus introduces us to provides a habitat for quick-growing shoots, but lacks the depth needed to sustain life. This person responds with "joy" after hearing the word, but the apparent change withers under the rays of the hot sun of distress or persecution (Matt. 13:20–21).

Most people within our contemporary Western church communities have experienced very little overt persecution for their faith. However, Jesus doesn't restrict falling away to the product of cultural or government sanctions, but also includes affliction, distress, and trouble. The cost of following Jesus is high, and it is high in ways often not seen.

We should never forget the amount of suffering we often call our friends and counselees to endure. It's difficult to be meek in a rancorous age. It's difficult to say "no" to deeply rooted sexual desires when being on the "right side of history" is clamoring for you to gratify them. It's hard to end a relationship that's dishonoring to Christ. It's hard to stand up to children's sinful desires, when reprisals of anger and sulking might undermine the family's equilibrium.

In these moments many plants begin to wilt. Many people take the first few steps for change, compelled by a new doctrinal discovery, unpleasant current circumstances, a genuine desire to change, or the insistence of a spouse, supervisor, or friend. There may be immediate growth as excitement or necessity compels immediate changes of behavior. But because the origin of that change wasn't God's grace, the thin silt at the top of the rocky soil could not provide the nourishment needed to sustain the change. What first appeared as fertile soil turned out to be a graveyard for change. Only grace-driven change will overcome these trials.

Seed #3: Choked by the Weeds

The third kind of soil we see is genuinely fertile. The seed germinates and, unlike the seed that fell in the rocky soil, has everything it needs to reach maturity. However, the seed falls victim to competition. Other seeds carried into the field by wind or animals sprout up alongside the seedling and ultimately crowd out an otherwise healthy plant.

Why is it that high school students who genuinely look to have a love for the Lord and are growing strongly wind up abandoning the Lord while at their university? Why does a couple that starts off putting in the hard work to grow their marriage wind up falling back into the old and easy habits? Why do movies, careers, sporting events, and a litany of other good things crowd out practically working to endure in transformation?

Anyone may live in ways that have every appearance of being faithful. And yet, when something tantalizing comes along that we have not yet encountered, the pursuit of growth and change is tested. As seen in the overgrown crops of Jesus' parable, many weeds will prove to be better suited to the soil of the heart than the good plants.

Overgrowth doesn't happen only when someone abandons the faith. It's a present feature of the smaller changes believers are called to make as well. We start full of passion and fervor, only to grow more interested in other comforts than in the hard work of cultivation. One counselee found himself addicted to his cell phone. He would do well for about two weeks, then fall back into the same habits. This happened time and again. Eventually, it became evident that the pleasures of reading news articles outstripped the desire to put the device aside and be present with his family. Those two-week spurts were driven by self and not the Savior. Only grace will enable a plant to outgrow the weeds.

Seed #4: The Flourishing Seed

The fourth seed is marked by enduring faithfulness. The plant arrives at maturity and bears much fruit. Any plant that completes the long journey from seed to seed-bearing has survived many obstacles. It has dodged the voracious birds, with a thousand falling on its right hand and left. It has endured the scorching sun because of the depths of its root, drinking deep of cool water when the rays might have wilted it. It has outgrown the weeds, defying their attempts to rob all the nutrients in the soil or block out the sun needed for photosynthesis. Indeed, the first psalm uses the picture of a plant to explain what a mature Christian looks like:

> *He is like a tree planted beside flowing streams*
> *that bears its fruit in its season,*
> *and its leaf does not wither.*
> *Whatever he does prospers.*
>
> *(Ps. 1:3)*

One of my favorite things about being a counselor is seeing the amount of change that the Lord uses me to bring into the lives of people. Just as the fruit borne by the mature plants will spawn grand-seeds after grand-seeds as each generation in turn produces fruit, so too does the growth of the heart in one individual often change the lives of those around them. A husband and wife whose poisonous marriage transforms to life-giving water have likely just changed their children's view of marriage. An individual whose lack of financial discipline weighs down his family materially, emotionally, and spiritually may become a wise handler of the resources God has loaned him. What a difference this will make in his own life and in the lives he is able to assist in transforming now that he is no longer simply living for himself! I will never fully see the generational impact of the fruit born out of my work to help others change. Neither will you. But how sweet it is to be part of God's plan to sanctify his people. Joy begets further joy.

We Are All Every Soil

When we step back and compare our lives with this parable, undoubtedly we notice that no one type of soil occupies the whole expanse of our hearts. By God's grace, there is much tilled and fertile soil in me. There is in you, too. But there are also plenty of rocky outcroppings, hard-packed paths, and pesky patches of fast-growing weeds. The truth is, every Christian is all four soils.

The good news is that God owns a rototiller to break up stubborn dirt clods, a pair of garden gloves to yank up thorns, a wheelbarrow to haul away stones, and a shotgun to deal with the birds. Slowly but surely, he is transforming the fields of our hearts into places that bear much fruit. Our hearts are more fertile now than they were when we first experienced the new birth. One day, the garden tools will be retired as we enter into the glory of the new earth. One day, there will be no more clods to till, no more weeds to pull, and no more stones to haul.

Endnotes

1. Bruce E. Wampold, *The Basics of Psychotherapy: An Introduction to Theory and Practice*, 2nd ed., Theories of Psychotherapy Series, ed. Jon Carlson and Matt Englar-Carlson (Washington, DC: American Psychological Association, 2019), 19–20.
2. Second Helvetic Confession, Article VII.
3. Frances Turretin highlights the distinction between spiritual regeneration and the regeneration of the body: "A 'new heart' is said to be made in us by regeneration not physically, but morally. The same substance which was corrupted by sin must be restored by grace." Frances Turretin, *Institutes of Elenctic Theology*, trans. George Musgrave Giger, ed. James T. Dennison, Jr. (Phillipsburg: P&R, 1992), 1.637.
4. Thomas Watson, *A Body of Divinity*, rev. ed. (Carlisle: Banner of Truth, 1965), 115.
5. I am indebted to my mentor, Jeremy Pierre, for the overall shape and argument of this section. See Jeremy Pierre, "Trust in the Lord with All Your Heart: The Centrality of Faith in Christ to the Restoration of Human Functioning" (PhD diss., The Southern Baptist Theological Seminary, 2010), 24–66, for a detailed exploration of the relationship of the terms soul, spirit, mind, and heart in the Hebrew and Greek Scriptures.
6. "*Psuche*," in *Theological Dictionary of the New Testament*, ed. G. Kittel, vol. 9 (Grand Rapids: Eerdmans, 1977), 639. Pierre notes, "As the proportion of the various meanings of [*psuche*] in the NT suggests, it is a term that is more regularly used to refer to the status of a person as a living being." Pierre, "Trust in the Lord," 54.
7. Pierre, "Trust in the Lord," 61.
8. For heart and mind see Deut. 11:18; 1 Sam. 2:35; 1 Chron. 22:19; 28:9; 2 Chron. 6:38; Job 38:36; Ps. 26:2; Jer. 11:20; 17:10; 20:12; 32:41; Matt. 22:37; Mark 12:30; Luke 10:27; Acts 4:32; Rom. 8:27; Phil. 4:7; Heb. 8:10; 10:16; James 4:8; Rev. 2:23. For soul and spirit see Job 7:11; 1 Thess. 5:23; Heb. 4:12.
9. A. Craig Troxel, *With All Your Heart: Orienting Your Mind, Desires, and Will toward Christ* (Wheaton, IL: Crossway, 2020), 32. John Calvin notes the same regarding the soul and spirit: "Now I understand by the term 'soul' an immortal yet created essence.... Sometimes it is called 'spirit.' For even when these terms are joined together, they differ from one another in meaning; yet when the word 'spirit' is used by itself, it means the same thing as soul" (John Calvin, *Institutes of the Christian Religion*, vol. 1, ed. John T. McNeill, trans. Ford Lewis Battles [Louisville, KY: Westminster John Knox, 1960], 1.15.2). Calvin's

talk of different meanings indicates what we have here described by "windows." The two terms are synonymous in what they indicate, but divergent in what they highlight.

10. The closest rival to "heart" is the term "mind." The Bible also frequently urges people to change their "minds," meaning to turn from wickedness to righteousness. However, the term "mind" is a more restrictive term than "heart," referring primarily to man's ability to reason and think. The heart, by contrast, includes thought but extends much further in its description of the human person.
11. Anthony A. Hoekema, "The Centrality of the Heart: A Study in Christian Anthropology with Special Reference to the Psychology of Herman Bavinck" (ThD thesis, Princeton Theological Seminary, 1948), 295.
12. Hoekema, "Centrality of the Heart," 295.
13. John Calvin set the trajectory for the traditional Reformed understanding by writing that the "soul consists of two faculties, understanding and will," where "will" included desiring and choosing abilities. Theologians such as Francis Turretin, Wilhelmus à Brakel, and Jonathan Edwards followed Calvin's lead. Other theologians elevated desiring into its own category, usually called the "affections." This can be seen in the works of John Owen, James Petigru Boyce, and Anthony Hoekema. Although the classifications are different, both streams of thought acknowledge the existence and importance of man's reasoning, desiring, and choosing capacities. For further study and detailed citations, see Nathanael Brooks, "Love the Lord with All Your Heart: The Defective Heart Psychology of Second-Wave Cognitive Behavioral Therapy" (PhD diss., Southwestern Baptist Theological Seminary, 2019), 47–95.
14. All emphasis in Scripture quotations has been added.
15. Hoekema, "Centrality of the Heart," 317.
16. Jeremy Pierre helpfully expands, "The necessary interrelatedness of the heart's functions compels the counselor to address each of these functions as interdependent upon the others. Emphasizing one aspect without due attention to the others will lead to a lopsided view of people and a lopsided methodology in handling them. The cognitive, affective, and volitional ought not be treated in isolation from one another. The human heart should not be addressed merely cognitively. Understanding helpful propositions, even those revealed in Scripture, is insufficient if it does not lead to affective and volitional conformity. An exclusively-didactic style of counseling that focuses on knowledge can be in danger of not paying adequate attention to a counselee's emotional responses as a vital aspect of their heart's response to God. It can also overlook the need to call a person volitionally to decision and prolonged dedication." Pierre, "Trust in the Lord," 220–221.
17. Petrus van Mastricht highlights the absolute necessity of guarding God's immutability: "God, and indeed only God, is entirely and in all ways immutable. . . . Amidst all the changes and vicissitudes, so many and so great, of the whole universe, he stands unmoved, and wholly unmovable. . . . [This] directs us to despise all creatures, however stable and brilliant they seem, when we consider that God is immutable." Petrus van Mastricht, *Theological-Practical Theology* (Grand Rapids, MI: Reformation Heritage, 2019), 2.155, 161.

Theologically considered, all creation is in a consistent state of change. An unbeliever is simply restricted in what kinds of change he or she can experience, not barred from all forms of change and thus rendered immutable. Certainly those arguing that unbelievers cannot change are not alleging they are immutable. However, reckless language often reflects poorly considered theology.

18. Part II of Jonathan Edwards' classic *Religious Affections* demonstrates how changes in affections, however strong they may be, can be sourced from different motivations. For example, an individual may have a strong "appearance of love" in his or her religious affections. Such strong love, however, is little proof of saving grace because it can be counterfeited. Edwards notes, "Christian love to the people of God may be counterfeited. It is evident by the Scripture, that there may be strong affections of this kind, without saving grace; as there were in the Galatians toward the apostle Paul, when they were ready to pluck out their eyes and give them to him; although the apostle expresses his fear that their affections were come to nothing and that he had bestowed upon them labor in vain." Jonathan Edwards, *A Treatise on Religious Affections*, in *The Works of Jonathan Edwards* (Peabody: Hendrickson, 2007), 250.
19. See Hoekema, "Centrality of the Heart," 314.
20. John Frame explores the totality of this corruption: "Continuing sin is, first of all, a heart condition. We have seen that the heart is the 'center' of our being, the inner disposition that governs all our thoughts, words, and deeds. . . . To speak of corruption at the level of the heart is to speak of a 'sinful nature,' a moral 'deadness.' As a dead man cannot get up and walk around, so a morally dead person cannot do works pleasing to God." John Frame, *Systematic Theology: An Introduction to Christian Belief* (Phillipsburg: P&R, 2013), 860.
21. Westminster Confession of Faith 16.7, Modern English Study Version. Available from the Orthodox Presbyterian Church at https://opc.org/documents/MESV_frames.html.
22. See Frame, *Systematic Theology*, 865–871.
23. Jesus uses the kindness of unbelievers to their children as an illustration of the Father's superabundant goodness toward believers in Matt. 7:7–11. A hungry child will not be given a rock or a snake, even though his parent is "evil" (7:11).
24. For a helpful discussion of the role of habits in sin and righteousness, see Brian Mesimer, "Rehabilitating Habituation," *Journal of Biblical Counseling* 34, no. 2 (2020): 53–79.
25. C. F. Keil offers penetrating analysis into the meaning of Judah's return in pretense only: "Although Josiah had put an end to the idol-worship, and though the people too, in the enthusiasm for the service of Jahveh [Yahweh], awakened by the solemn celebration of the passover [*sic*], had broken in pieces the images and altars of the false gods throughout the land, yet there was imminent danger that the people, alienated in heart from the living God, should take the suppression of open idolatry for a true return to God, and, vainly admiring themselves, should look upon themselves as righteous and pious. Against this delusion the prophet takes his stand." C. F. Keil, *Jeremiah, Lamentations*, Keil-Delitzsch Commentary on the Old Testament in Ten Volumes (Grand Rapids, MI: Eerdmans, repr. 1978), 7.87–88. Although he does not use the language of operation and

orientation change, Keil points out that the people have indeed enthusiastically rid themselves of open idolatry, yet confused their zeal for actual love to Yahweh.

26. See Wampold, *Basics of Psychotherapy*, 67–89, for a helpful summary of the impulses, findings, and disputed interpretations of empirical research in historical and contemporary psychotherapeutic techniques.
27. The work of secular psychologist Jerome Frank has been particularly effective in demonstrating that most major forms of secular therapy aid clients with the same frequency (J. D. Frank, "Therapeutic Factors in Psychotherapy," *American Journal of Psychotherapy* 25 no. 3 [1971]: 350–361). See also Wampold, *Basics of Psychotherapy*, 70–72; Mark R. McMinn, Stanton L. Jones, Michael J. Vogel, and Richard E. Butman, "Cognitive Therapy," in *Modern Psychotherapies: A Comprehensive Christian Appraisal*, ed. Stanton L. Jones and Richard E. Butman, 2nd ed. (Downers Grove, IL: IVP Academic, 2011), 201–260 (250).
28. For a helpful and comprehensive list of the various terms the Scriptures use for regeneration, see James Petigru Boyce, *Abstract of Systematic Theology* (Cape Coral, FL: Founders Press, 2006), 374.
29. Charles Hodge, *Systematic Theology* (Peabody, MA: Hendrickson, 2013), 3.5.
30. See Thomas Goodwin, *Unregenerate Man's Guiltiness*, in *The Works of Thomas Goodwin*, vol. 3 (Edinburgh: James Nichol, 1861–1866; repr. Eureka, CA: Tanski Publications, 1996), 10.137; Wilhelmus à Brakel, *The Christian's Reasonable Service*, vol. 1, trans. Bartel Elshout (Ligonier, PA: Soli Deo Gloria, 1992), 320.
31. See William G. T. Shedd, *Dogmatic Theology* (Phillipsburg, NJ: P&R, 2003), 510–520.
32. Louis Berkhof, *Systematic Theology* (Grand Rapids, MI: Eerdmans, 2018), 468.
33. Van Mastricht, *Theological-Practical Theology*, 341.
34. Berkhof, *Systematic Theology*, 469.
35. See Berkhof, *Systematic Theology*, 468, for a helpful discussion.
36. There are typically three different aspects to sanctification: positional sanctification, progressive sanctification, and final sanctification. For the purposes of this short work we are considering only progressive sanctification, as it is the aspect most relevant to the process of heart change.
37. Watson, *Body of Divinity*, 241.
38. Ibid.
39. An extended discussion of the nuts and bolts of sanctification falls outside the scope of our current study. Thankfully, we are blessed by many excellent works on this topic. My personal favorite is David Powlison, *How Does Sanctification Work?* (Wheaton, IL: Crossway, 2017). See also Tim Chester, *You Can Change* (Wheaton, IL: Crossway, 2008); and Jim Newheiser, *Help! I Want to Change* (Wapwallopen, PA: Shepherd Press, 2014).

40. Kevin DeYoung, "Spirit-Powered, Gospel-Driven, Faith-Fueled Effort" (plenary address, Together for the Gospel Conference, Louisville, KY, April 10–12, 2012), https://t4g.org/resources/kevin-deyoung/spirit-powered-gospel-driven-faith-fueled-effort-2.
41. Van Mastricht, *Theological-Practical Theology*, 420. Punctuation lightly edited for clarity.
42. David Powlison, *God's Grace in Your Suffering* (Wheaton, IL: Crossway, 2018), 82–83.
43. Within the different approaches to therapy and counseling, biblical counseling is uniquely situated as being a means of sanctification due to its emphasis on the wise application of the Scriptures to life in concert with help from a wise counselor.
44. I have changed this friend's name for the sake of his privacy, though he has given me permission to share his story.
45. David L. Turner, *Matthew*, Baker Exegetical Commentary on the New Testament (Grand Rapids, MI: Baker Academic, 2008), 410–411.
46. I'm grateful to Dr. Jonathan Pennington for this piece of cultural knowledge.
47. Philip Graham Ryken, *Galatians*, Reformed Expository Commentary Series (Phillipsburg, NJ: P&R, 2005), 56.
48. David and Krista Dunham, *Table for Two: Biblical Counsel for Eating Disorders* (Greensboro, NC: New Growth Press), 6.
49. St. Ignatius, "The Epistle of Ignatius to the Romans," New Advent, https://www.newadvent.org/fathers/0107.htm.
50. George M. Marsden, *Jonathan Edwards: A Life*, read by Jim Denison (Ashland, OR: Blackstone Audio, 2018), 24 hr., 29 min. Jonathan Edwards' legacy as a theologian is certainly sullied by his endorsement of and participation in chattel slavery. Knowing this, I have still decided to use his work extensively in this chapter because of the clarity and precision of *Religious Affections*. Shai Linne provides what I think is a careful and helpful discussion of how to wisely engage with confessionally orthodox but morally compromised theologians in chapter 4 of Shai Linne, *The New Reformation* (Chicago: Moody Press, 2021).
51. Edwards, *Religious Affections*.
52. C. S. Lewis, *The Great Divorce* (1946; repr., New York: Macmillan, 1965), 99–101.
53. Watson, *Body of Divinity*, 241.
54. D. A. Carson, *Matthew 13–28*, The Expositor's Bible Commentary (Grand Rapids, MI: Zondervan, 1995), 313.

About Shepherd Press Publications

- They are gospel driven.
- They are heart focused.
- They are life changing.

Our Invitation to You

We passionately believe that what we are publishing can be of benefit to you, your family, your friends, and your work colleagues. So we are inviting you to join our online mailing list so that we may reach out to you with news about our latest and forthcoming publications, and with special offers.

Visit:

www.shepherdpress.com/newsletter

and provide your name and email address.